# a LEGACY of DAYS

## Ten Fun Ways to Tell Your Story to the Next Generation

## LETITIA SUK

FUSION
HYBRID PUBLISHING

A Legacy of Days: Ten Fun Ways to Tell Your Story to the Next Generation

End Game Press books may be purchased in bulk at special discounts for sales promotion, corporate gifts, ministry, fund-raising, or educational purposes. Special editions can also be created to specifications. For details, contact Special Sales Dept., End Game Press, P.O. Box 206, Nesbit, MS 38651 or info@endgamepress.com.

Visit our website at www.endgamepress.com.

HB: 9781637972540
PB ISBN: 9781637972557
eBook ISBN: 9781637972564

Cover by Cassidy Wierks, Typewriter Creative
Interior Design by PerfecType, Nashville, TN

Printed in the United States of America
10 9 8 7 6 5 4 3 2 1

*To my eleven grandchildren, the start of the next generation.*

*Aaliyah, Judah, Lydia*
*Nayshawn and Marshawn*
*Camila, Evan, and Julian*
*Tommy, Irene, and Betty*

# CONTENTS

# INTRODUCTION
## Everyone Has a Story

"Find anything yet?" I shouted across the small country grave-yard to my brother, Mark. We were on another one of our cem-etery crawls, trying to locate the final resting places of relatives we had never met. Despite walking up and down the uneven rows for some time, no luck had shown up.

I don't remember how this started, but as often is the case with adult sibs, one day we realized we shared an avid interest. We both had been peeking into the early history of our family. I remember laughing when we discovered our mutual fascination and felt delighted to find something new about someone I grew up with.

Like emptying our pockets on the table, we started compar-ing the information and details we had found on our forays into the past. Neither one of us had a lot of findings, but together it was a more impressive cache. Mark still lives in the town where we grew up, so we decided to join forces sleuthing for family clues during my then-monthly visits to our mom.

## MY STORY

On this sunny April day, we scavenged the countryside for the tomb of our great-great-grandmother, Christina Flick Schwartz. The GPS on our smartphones didn't seem equipped for this old church cemetery that wasn't anywhere near the church. We kept following country roads as they appeared and felt like gold diggers when we found the location.

I only first heard about our ancestor Christina a few months before the day of our explorations. One of our cousins who shares our enthusiasm about family history filled me in on her name and where she was buried. The small cemetery is located about thirty minutes outside of our hometown, an easy excursion.

I don't have memories of my mom ever mentioning Christina, her great-grandmother. Like generations before her, my mother grew up on a farm. Seems like the never-ending tasks of the present day occupied all the available time, so they had little opportunity to reflect on the past. Or maybe no one talked about her because there was nothing to say since she left no story. All I knew was she was the mother of the first Schwartz Family (my mother's family) to come to the United States from Germany in 1873.

Heinrich, Christina's husband, had already been located on another adventure. Funny thing, Heinrich was buried in a different cemetery! When Christina died thirty-seven years after Heinrich, the creek by the cemetery where he was buried had flooded, making the roads impassable. Her body had to be taken to this cemetery instead. I imagine that caused a lot of last-minute chaos in making sure everyone knew where to go!

"I think I found it!" I yelled across the tombstones. There it was right in front of me, a simple white headstone engraved with her birth year, 1837, and her death year, 1912. My heart pounded as I touched the weathered stone. Here she was.

I stood and stared at the stone, longing for so much more detail. I felt bereft that my family had no stories, no clues, nothing to fill me in on this woman. I wanted a protected envelope on the back of the stone that filled in all the events between those two dates. Isn't that a great idea if those existed?

"Who were you? What were you like?" I spoke to Christina as though she could hear me, needing a place to direct my burning questions.

## HISTORY

All I knew was that Christina left Germany, the land of her birth, and boarded a ship at some point to sail over the ocean to America. Finding her grave only fueled my desire to learn more.

I assumed she was a farmer's wife, so I could fill in a few blanks in my imagination. Long days on her feet, many meals to prepare for her large family, chickens to tend, eggs to gather.

From my reading of *Little House on the Prairie* by Laura Ingalls Wilder, I could fill in more imaginary details as it covers a similar time period. Cows to milk. Quilts to piece. Food to plant, tend, harvest, and store for the winter added to her day-to-day work.

What were her days like? Who were her neighbors? Did she have friends? How did she feel about leaving Germany? *Tell me about the boat ride, Christina . . . Did you get seasick? What was it like here in those years after the Civil War?* Maybe she kept a diary. *Wouldn't that be fun to find!*

I knew she bore seven children—at least that number lived. During that time, many families lost children in infancy. One of her children was my great-grandfather, Frank, whom I never met. What was he like? Another story I would like to know.

We piled back in the car, but all the questions remained. I thought about Christina for a long time after that day.

I resolved not to do that to future generations. Leave no story, just dates on a tombstone. It feels like my mandate, my duty. Two hundred years from now if someone goes looking for me, wonders what I was like, I want to be found. Story intact, more or less. But how? Perhaps the better question is *why*.

Each of us might answer that question in a different way. Some are interested just for fun; genealogy is a fast-growing hobby. Others want to identify the box of photos they inherited from their grandparents. Medical mysteries are another reason— looking for family connections to physical traits or illness.

My answer to the *why* question? I want the days of my life to count not just for this life but to all who follow. Especially to impact and influence those who do and will carry traces of my DNA. To take my place in my family line of "begats" just like the genealogy lists in the Bible, only with more than just a name.

So much of my story is more about what God has done in my life rather than where I went to school. I want my future generations to also know the Lord's goodness I have experienced, and I believe God wants that too.

I hope someone cares about what I love and how I spend my time, the opinions and values I hold, and my highest hopes for all my descendants because, of course, I have them. We tell our story to be known but also to help others know themselves. Our story is never just ours. It overlaps and belongs to all who share this segment of life's path with us.

Story is powerful. People remember narrative details far longer than facts. Stories can showcase an individual or family, but also invite the reader to find himself or herself in the listening. Although everyone has a story, without intentionality all memories will be lost. Someone has to write it down. What is not written is not remembered.

## GOD'S STORY

Tales have been around since the beginning of time. Long before cave wall drawings and hieroglyphics of ancient Egypt, stories passed much the same way they do now, one generation telling the next. I was surprised to find out the famous "Aesop Fables" were not written until 300 years after Aesop's death around 564 BC. Oral tradition kept them alive.

Bible genealogy records indicate this is important to God too. Whole chapters in the Old Testament and several sections in the New Testament offer long lists of family lineage. It is easy to skim these chapters, but each of these names and their place in history is significant to God as well as their families. Your name is on a list like that somewhere.

In the genealogies listed in Ezra 2:62, one group *"searched for their family records, but they could not find them and so were excluded from the priesthood as unclean."* Whoops! Don't want to lose track of those records.

The whole of Joshua 4 includes detailed instruction about setting up a pile of stones to remember what God has done. *"These stones are to be a memorial to the people of Israel forever . . . so that all the peoples of the earth might know that the hand of the LORD is powerful and so that you might always fear the LORD your*

*God"* (vv. 7b, 24). Seems clear that God wants us to remember our stories too, especially the ones that involve Him.

I love the introduction to the Gospel of Luke where Luke explains why he wrote the account of Jesus' life. *"Many have undertaken to draw up an account of the things that have been fulfilled among us, just as they were handed down to us by those who from the first were eyewitnesses and servants of the word. With this in mind, since I myself have carefully investigated everything from the beginning, I too decided to write an orderly account for you, most excellent Theophilus, so that you may know the certainty of the things you have been taught"* (Luke 1:1-4).

## YOUR STORY

All of us have been shaped in some way by the stories of individuals we are not related to and have never met. At parties or small group meetings, when the ice-breaker question is asked, "Who influenced you the most, living or dead?" many of us name someone we have never met but know about through their story. And how do we know these stories? Because they are preserved from one generation to the next.

Your ancestor might not be a queen, an inventor, or a famous evangelist, but they too have a story to tell that has a direct link to your life. Do you ever wish you knew more about them or how they spent their days? If not yet, you will likely feel this desire even stronger when you grow older and see the next generations of your family arriving.

The lifespan of the average person living today is about 32,000 days. Wouldn't you like your descendants to know at least some of those days? Telling your story gives you the opportunity to speak into lives you will never meet.

As the psalmist wrote, *"Let this be written for a future generation, that a people not yet created my praise the* LORD*"* (Psalm 102:18).

As for my own story, my lifelong fascination for all things historical propels me to raise my hand when family memorabilia go up for grabs. "I'll take it." I guess that makes me the family historian.

Archives and artifacts, mostly photos but papers as well, of both sides of my family and some of my husband's family are now mine to process, preserve, and pass on. The piles grew as I discovered new troves of data each time I looked around my mom's basement. Can you relate?

Meanwhile, I am also keeping track of my day-to-day life through journals, letters, memorabilia, scrapbooks, calendars, and the like. I am not a packrat when it comes to stuff, but if there is such a thing as a memorabilia packrat, I qualify. Most of us save at least a few things to remind us of things, places, or people we love. Don't you?

Of course, what I want to pass on is not the *stuff* but the *story*. Quilts, dishes, and jewelry are lovely mementos from the past but don't tell a story if no one knows their origins. I have those items too, cherish them, and will pass them on. Hopefully, because of my efforts, with more information about the women who first owned them.

We can't presume—or worse yet, insist—that our children or theirs will be interested, but we can provide the opportunity. Not by handing over boxes and bags and a cache of photos, but by finding a way to tell the story that not only works but is enjoyable.

Don't worry. This is not meant to be an exhaustive list of how-to, but more of a menu for a place to start. You will find that you are already doing a few of them without calling them "telling your story." Even if you don't have relatives, do it for yourself.

Thumb through the book, try on which methods sound interesting, and see what fits. Some will, some won't. Please don't try to do them all at once. Make sure you are having fun along the way.

When we know our story, we know ourselves.

## WHAT TO EXPECT

As you move through the following chapters, you will notice that each method of storytelling opens with introductory information:

- How does it tell our story?
- Degree of difficulty?
- Amount of time?
- Cost?

At the conclusion of each chapter, you will also find:

- FAQ about the chapter concept.
- Vignettes from contributors which show how others use the method.
- How about you? Several questions to lead you into trying out the method.

Ready to jump in? Let's go!

# ONE

## The Family Life Journal

---

### HOW DOES IT TELL OUR STORY?
A short, written account of how we spent each day.

### DEGREE OF DIFFICULTY?
Low

### AMOUNT OF TIME?
Two to three minutes each day.

### COST?
None other than the cost of the diary.

---

I wish I could remember how the conversation started. My mug of strong black tea laced with milk sat on the tray and my journal lounged in my lap, just like every morning. My eleven-year-old granddaughter was draped over another chair, also with a book in hand. We flitted between writing, reading, and chitchatting.

Somehow Texas came up in our random morning-after-sleepover conversation, which segued into my brother's long-ago Texas wedding.

"Something happened to our car on that trip," I mused.

"What was that?" Of course, she didn't know.

We both glanced at the glass-door bookcase in the corner. Lined up neatly on the second shelf sat the colorful spines of the journals that hold our family memories. Twenty-eight volumes and counting. We would soon know the rest of that story.

A quick grab of Journal #1 revealed the whole account of the brief demise of our van on a lonesome Sunday in Nowhere, Texas, as we headed home from that wedding.

I read the account aloud to my granddaughter.

"We stopped at a McDonald's drive-thru for breakfast. Right after we left there, the van started vibrating, and we realized we were in trouble. Then we remembered it was Sunday in Texas and nothing would be open. Of course, we prayed and sure enough we found an open Western Auto shop. While we waited for the repair, we read, did homework, and tried to keep busy. We were on the road again by 11:00 a.m."

The Family Life Journal delivered again. Thirty-six years of jotting a few lines to remember each day now filled in the story when only a vague memory flashed across. My only regret was that I didn't start recording earlier.

## THE FAMILY LIFE JOURNAL

Have you noticed how some seasons of our lives swoop by so fast that scant tangible memories remain? Childhood, both mine and now my children's, have great gaps in the narrative. Hard to believe I spent a full year in fourth grade and can remember only one thing about it: finding out the "real" first name of my favorite nun was Alice. The same is true of the other early years—just a smattering of memories.

Most of the rest of us can rewind movies in our heads of a handful of highlights of childhood. Vacations or special events are often recalled more vividly. Perhaps memories of trips and holidays are more remembered as they were a change of venue from the familiar day in/day out of ordinary life. Photographs also fill in stories.

As we age, a selective amnesia of sorts sets in when new experiences crowd out older memories. To remember the details of most moments of our lives would be overwhelming. In fact, there is a medical term for those rare individuals who can call to mind almost every detail of their lives: hyperthymia or HSAM (highly superior autobiographical memory). Can you imagine knowing what you had for lunch on May 19 seventeen years ago?

Intentionally storing key moments or events in our lives can shape not only our own identity, but also that of our family. Have you ever noticed all the references woven throughout the Bible with the instruction to "Write this down" or "Remember this?" I believe God wants us to live with the next generation in mind by remembering and passing the stories on.

But how? It hardly seemed possible to add one more item to the never-ending to-do list of life with young children. Many days it was enough to just get through the day, much less try to hang on to the highlights or write anything down about it.

I remember random details and haven't forgotten the labors and deliveries and could tell you all the minute-by-minute action even now (but I won't). Some things you never forget.

I did keep a prayer journal of sorts in that early season where I would write my prayers, my angst, my spiritual ups and downs, but it was "write as needed" without much day-to-day detail.

Day after day flowed by in what I call the long "blur" season of my life. I often wondered what any of us would remember about these days of playing house for real. We spent so much of our together time making lunches, preparing dinner, cleaning up, tossing another load of laundry in, and . . . you know how it goes.

Don't get me wrong, I loved the delightful time with my precious ones and knew deep foundations were being laid, but my slow days moved fast. As Gretchen Rubin wrote in *The Happiness Project*, "The days are long, but the years are short."* Often, I would murmur, "I won't forget this" after some poignant or exciting moment, but I did.

## AN ACTION PLAN

My angst about losing the moments came to a head one day on October 15, 1988, a most random, nondescript day ten years after our first child was born. A splash of "free time" must have shown up, enough to entertain an innovative thought. Most of my creative thinking channeled into the daily conundrum of what to make for dinner. A struggle that continues to this day.

Somewhere in the gap that day between school's end and dinner prep's beginning, the idea danced into my mind to start recording the *ordinary* events of the day beginning with *today*, instead of the beginning of the month, next week, whenever.

---

* Gretchen Rubin, *The Happiness Project* (New York, NY: HarperCollins, 2009), 97.

Not another journal to process life or capture feelings, but a way to capture our corporate experience as a family.

I'm convinced that if I'd decided to first start one more load of laundry or add another plate to the dishwasher, the idea would have receded for another six and a half years or so. Some ideas need action NOW.

I herded the four kids, ages two to ten, into our van and drove to the closest bookstore to buy a blank book. Mom on a mission! My idea was to record the events of each day in a couple of sentences. Enough to catch the highlights, but not too much to get overwhelmed by the task. I knew it had to be a low time commitment to maintain.

## A FRESH JOURNAL

My creativity fizzles at night, so I waited until the next morning to begin. I already had a carved-out time for prayer each day, which varied from ten to twenty minutes, so adding the new practice to that time made sense instead of looking for another slot.

On the front page of the book, I inscribed:

"To my children, so you may know what your mother was like and how we lived our lives together when you were growing up."

Then I jotted a couple lines about what we did the day before:

"Dad and I spoke at a marriage conference and Karla took the older kids to the Art Institute. Christa was next door at the Cooneys' all day. We ordered pizza from Little Caesars and ate it sitting on the floor watching the first game of the World Series. Dodgers vs Oakland A's."

For the past thirty-six years, I haven't stopped.

In less than two minutes each morning, I can record the events of the previous day in three to four lines. Most days are not that sensational! The entries are all about the facts, the classic *who, what, where, when*, and occasionally *why*. I might include the weather or the dinner entrée, but rarely any emotion other than a descriptive word, such as "fun, exciting, challenging, etc."

Keeping it simple keeps me coming back each day. I save the drama for my prayer journal.

Funny, but the journals have evolved into our family's Google system. Questions like "Who did I go to prom with junior year?" "When did I get braces?" "Where did we go on vacation in 1993?" are all answered in the readily available volumes.

"Mom, check the book" is a phrase that often comes my way as my adult children are looking back to their childhood. Many family wonderings or disagreements have been settled by going back to the source. The plan worked; the days were remembered.

## A HABIT FORMED

I hope to keep this practice up for, let's say, another thirty years. Maybe no one will care that one day we ordered pizza and watched a ball game. Could be said about many days around here! But I care. And that is enough. And you care . . . and that is all that matters for you too.

I opened the family journal this morning to record a few lines about yesterday:

"Went to church, uploaded vacation photos, dropped off a birthday gift of a turquoise backpack to our granddaughter, made pumpkin soup for Sunday night dinner, and watched 60 Minutes."

Short, simple, satisfying.

Much of history we know from personal journals. Think about Anne Frank's daily entries of her life in hiding from the Nazis in Amsterdam. Meriwether Lewis's account of the details of the Lewis and Clark Expedition to the Pacific in the early 1800s. Mary Chesnut's diary of domestic life during the Civil War, which was used as part of the narrative for filmmaker Ken Burns's documentary of this era.

If you aren't writing your story in some fashion, who is? I'm counting on someone in my family benefitting from my efforts and keeping the story going, but it's my turn now.

Once a year in the first week of the new year, I reread the past year in its entirety. Sometimes I make a game of the memories by quizzing my husband on what happened last February, April, etc. We have fun remembering and end up giving thanks to God for all the moments.

I do wonder what other ideas got away in that season of life, but so glad this one didn't.

## OTHER TYPES OF FAMILY LIFE JOURNALS

### Short-term Journals

Sometimes it is easier to make a commitment for a short-term journal. Maybe that feels more doable for you to try this method of telling your story without a long-term commitment. This modified journaling could work for any segment of time. To narrow it even more, try a travel journal for your next trip. I still have mine from a long time ago. Quite fascinating to read!

As an avid lover of summer, in 1975 I began a "Summer Journal" to keep track of my favorite ninety-nine days of the year. Once a day I would write an account of our goings-on that summer as so much activity seemed swirling around us.

I hardly recognize my day-to-day life back in the mid-seventies. Jobs as well as school for the two of us plus church planting with our team of nine filled out every calendar box. Pre-kids for us then like our current empty nest, but such different agenda for each day compared to now.

> July 2, 1975: "I picked up some lemonade and took it to the beach with our neighbor, Marianne. She bought me a hotdog and we talked for hours. Our friend, Phil, from church came for an early dinner. Later I visited an Indian couple, Purnima and Bob, whom I met at the laundromat. We had a nice visit and I invited them over next Tuesday."

The Summer Journals continued for many years, starting around Memorial Day, and finishing on Labor Day. Somehow, I didn't have the consistency problem that plagued my earlier attempts to capture the rhythms of life. Maybe because summer has so many fun moments to record!

About twelve years ago, I grabbed the earliest Summer Journal (1975) and brought it on our vacation. Each evening and during long drives I would read aloud from our early adventures. We enjoyed hearing the stories so much that we kept reading once we got home. Many long discussions resulted from taking this unique look at our early marriage.

Every year since, I have brought an old Summer Journal along on our vacation and continued the practice. Once we go through all the old Summer Journals, we will move on to a re-read of the Family Life Journals which took their place in 1988.

## HOLIDAY JOURNALS

Do you ever have a hard time remembering the details of how you celebrated Christmas in past years? Can you recall gifts you gave or received? Consider starting a unique Christmas Journal to capture the holiday memories of this treasured season.

Items to record could also include who you celebrated with, what was on the menu, what the weather was like, or any other special experiences you don't want to forget. My family still loves to remember our little two-year-old son singing "Jesus Loves Me" during a Christmas shopping outing. He has kids of his own now, and they love this story too.

Our Thanksgiving Journal also sits on the shelf with all the family journals and holds our annual lists of all the things we were thankful for covering the past thirty-five years. Included are the names of the individuals who sat around our table each year and how we spent the rest of the long weekend. See appendix 3 for more information on how to keep this journal. Perhaps Valentine's Day or Easter is celebrated significantly in your family. Keeping a journal with memories of those or other holidays would also be meaningful.

## BACK TO YOU

What if you discovered a journal like this that someone in your family started right around the age you are now? Wouldn't you be so eager to dig in? It is never too late to start recording the days.

Choose a style that feels like you and jump in with what happened in your daily round yesterday, today, last week. You will only regret not starting.

## FAQ ABOUT THE FAMILY LIFE JOURNAL

**Can't I just use my "regular" processing journal to keep track of the days?**

Yes, you can if that works for you. Consider, though, if you want your family to have access to these to browse or find answers to questions about past family experiences. Setting aside a designated "Family Life Journal" gives everyone access to information and memories without divulging your inner feelings you might not want to share.

**What if I get behind?**

Common concern and it does happen! Do your best to remember by looking at calendars, asking family members, etc. Sometimes a few entries are: "I don't remember."

**Why not include feelings/emotions in this record?**

Because it will slow you down and those feelings/emotions might change over time, but facts won't. I add adjectives like *fun, hard, sad*, etc. but I don't go into detail.

**What if I want to do a modified version?**

Do whatever style of journal will work for you. Try the travel, summer, or holiday version to get started. Another simple variation could be a Birthday Journal to keep track of each year's festivities.

## WHO ELSE IS RECORDING THE DAYS?

I asked a few friends to share their experiences with keeping an accounting of the days, here is what they reported:

--------

"I started using a daily five-year journal because I felt I had no system for marking time in our family life. Everything seemed like a blur that amounted to a lot of nothing. I don't love journaling, but I wanted a way to keep track of our days as a family. It's easy to keep up, especially since I'm not including commentary about emotions. I sometimes go back and write a few things down, but I give myself grace and leave some days blank if I forget to journal. Writing these lines helps me remember how we spent our time and various milestones. I hope it is a way for us to look back and see when things happened in our lives and how we spent our time."

—Heather Logue, 48, Skokie, Illinois, dean of residence life

--------

"I have been journaling for sixteen years and bullet journaling for about a year. I purposefully do not leave much room for the bullet sections of my journal because I want to keep it brief. Just a few things from my day that stand out by the time I go to bed—good things, bad things, funny and amusing moments, precious memories, etc. Basically, a little bit of everything. Of course, it varies day to day, but overall, the goal is just to mention a few things that made that day unique."

—Angela Cornell, 35, Indiana, content writer

--------

"I started journaling on a trip to the Boundary Waters in August of 2007. I knew it was something I didn't want to forget, so I wrote about it. I just kept going. I liked the idea of being able to look back on any day in my life to see what I had done. The way

I saw it, I could Google anything I wanted, but I could not do a Google search of my own experiences.

Even in a digital age, where we have thousands of blogs and pictures and video evidence, I felt like a daily chronicle would still leave a unique legacy for generations behind me to look back on. Within those journals, I have captured the daily life of living through high school and college, falling in love, and getting married, COVID, buying a house, and becoming a parent in the twenty-first century. It is mundane, but that is what makes it a unique study.

I know that I would have appreciated having something like this from my own parents, grandparents or even great-grandparents. Each year I order a printed, bound copy. If that is something I can pass on to even one person who finds it useful or even mildly interesting, then I am glad to do it."

—Dallas Rayburn, 31, Bloomer, Wisconsin,
high school English teacher

———

"I began this practice in January 2021, when we were very slowly starting to find a semblance of normalcy in life again after COVID, even as lockdowns continued. At that time my children were four and one. At age forty-two, in this season of life, all the rhythms I expected I'd have as a woman, wife, youth pastor, and mom to young children were different than what I had imagined. I knew people had been keeping lockdown journals in the early days, and I wanted to find a way to remember these quickly passing days, even if it was just one funny thing a child did, or one memorable walk to the playground.

I try to include one funny story or memorable moment, but there are days when I just can't think of one (especially if I'm updating it a week or more later), so then I just write factually about something that happened, even if it's the same as almost every other day (school, work, meetings, playground visit, etc.). This practice also forces me to stop and reflect on moments of the day, almost like an examen. I think about moments of joy we experienced, or even contentment, and try to record them.

Quite simply, the practice helps me remember these years that are flying by, even when they fly by at the speed of molasses! They are also a way to track important milestones in career, marriage, record what we do on vacations, and so forth. I use a five-year journal and like the snapshot you get on each page of five years in the life of a growing, changing family."

—Stephanie Fosnight Register, 45,
Evanston, IL, writer and editor

## HOW ABOUT YOU?

1. Have you ever kept an account of the days? Why did you stop? What kept you going?
2. What about the Family Life Journal appeals to you?
3. Are you interested in beginning now?
4. How would you like to see your written memories used in your family?

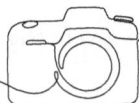

# TWO

## Storytelling with Photos

---

### HOW DOES IT TELL OUR STORY?
Provides images of faces and places to fill in details of our story.

### DEGREE OF DIFFICULTY?
Easy to moderate depending on obtaining
and identifying the photos.

### AMOUNT OF TIME?
Varied.

### COST?
Free to moderate if photo programs or services are used.

---

The warning across my phone screen set off multiple alarms: "You are almost out of photo storage space. Act immediately." A more techie-confident person might have known what to do. Faced with deleting or even sorting my precious photos, I chose the simplest option. Buy more storage!

Bring up photos and it's likely a collective groan will go off. We love them, but they can overwhelm us by the sheer quantity. However, technology offers an increasing supply of great options for dealing with photos in a way that enhances our storytelling possibilities.

At my fiftieth high school reunion, everyone pulled out their phones and paraded photos of their grandchildren around to their old friends in the room. Me too! In earlier times, we might have carried little photos in our wallets or envelopes in our purses. How convenient to have so many pictures right at hand! In fact, we have hundreds/thousands/more of these snapshots of memories.

In my youth, we stored photos in shoeboxes or envelopes, when we got around to getting the film developed. Today, they are all over our digital space as well and we add to our collection. Besides all the pictures on your phone or laptop, your photos might be on chips or sticks or CDs or all of the above.

Photos tell the story of our lives, who we are as a family, and they are one of the easiest ways to pass on a legacy of days. It is important to do that in an intentional way, though, so you are not just passing on an old box of unidentified relatives or worse yet, your phone or computer gets recycled along with the photos living on it. Lost forever. Scary, right?

We plan to organize our photos in some way to pass on the stories. "I'll get around to it." But do we? Then there is the stash of inherited-from-relatives photos gathering dust in a box somewhere. Often the story is all there, but the details are missing to fill it in. Who are these people in the pictures, and where are these locations? It isn't that we do not care, but there are so many mysteries to solve and the longer we wait, the harder they are to unravel.

Photos are one of the best ways to tell a family story and most of us own or have access to all the materials needed. How to get started is where we get stuck. The bigger question is why are you doing this? We all have countless demands on our time so why is this one getting priority now? Only you can answer that question.

## CAST A VISION

To tell your story with photos, start with the end goal in mind. If you finished sorting your photos, how would they be organized? Don't rush through this answer. If you are sorting them for the next generations, which way do you think works for them?

Do you want to first digitalize everything and go from there? Frame photos? Create handmade albums for your friends and family? Design digital albums? How about giving away photos? Identify people and places? Toss all the not-so-good ones? Keeping the finished product in mind can keep you on track so you are working on what will be meaningful to you, not just a project. Taking time to answer these questions may seem unnecessary but will pay off in the end.

## PLAN A PROJECT OVERVIEW

Adding a new project to your already full day-to-day life can seem daunting. Before jumping in, give thought to the plan of your project. Decide how often and when you will work on this. On weekends? Twenty minutes a day? While you watch TV? What will work for you?

Hopefully, you will feel the freedom not to have to get it all done immediately. On the other hand, a deadline might be a useful tool. Consider a finish line by the end of year or the

Fourth of July or by the time school starts or a date somewhat far away, but not too far to cause you to procrastinate.

## GET STARTED

What are ways to create a story with photos without drowning in them? Getting started is often the hardest task. There is no right way to jump in. Any place will work.

**Let's start with physical photos:** Gather all the ones you have in one place. Dining room table, basement floor, unused bed. Find a space where you can spread out. That includes those already in frames.

**Choose a sorting method that makes sense to you:** chronological, by person, by family, by event (Christmas, vacation, weddings, etc.). You can change the sorting themes along the way, but the important thing is to jump in and get started. Set aside all the "B" and below quality. You want to work with the best you have. Toss the blurred or un-identifiable.

Most of us probably have thousands of photos that could be tossed. It sounds ruthless but it is true. Do you need ALL the photos of Christmas morning twenty-two years ago? Wouldn't one tell the story?

**Decide which photos you want to edit, copy, or restore:** set those aside for now. If possible, keep sorting until you finish with this phase before starting any projects such as albums. Remember, even if it feels slow, you are still making more progress than you did before you started!

Hopefully, while you are sorting, you will begin to envision what you could do with the photos. You do not have to make anything permanent. Try to get into a playful mode like a kid building with blocks. See what happens!

If possible, leave your project out so you can come back to it without a lot of effort. The exception would be if you are making a gift or if you are concerned about unwanted comments by others who might see it. Creativity can be very fragile, and you do not want to get kiboshed.

## WAYS TO DISPLAY YOUR PHOTO STORIES

### Photo Albums

If making a photo album appeals to you, do you prefer a physical album or a digital one? How do you envision accessing this album? Both now and in the future.

Does artistry matter to you? Some photo albums are so beautiful yet can become almost intimidating. Maybe just getting it done is a higher value for you. I have a few old, falling-apart albums and am so grateful that the owner just did something instead of waiting for perfection!

On my photo album shelf, in addition to our family albums are my mother's albums and several from my grandparents. That generation is gone, but the pictures live on. Select photos are captioned, but many are not recognizable. I still enjoy browsing them.

How about you? Does anyone ever have a mental debate about making a digital book or handmade one? Although I prefer to make physical albums, I have designed several digital albums for family and friends. They are not as intimidating as they sound!

The first one was for my mom after a visit from her oldest great-grandson and me. After the trip I checked out one of the photo sites, and in about an hour, designed an album with the best photos from the trip for Christmas gifts.

Another set of albums started from a weekend away with my high school girlfriends. After minimal contact over the years as jobs, kids, and all the details of life took over, we spent a weekend together. The cameras snapped! Each of us took photos throughout the weekend and shared them with each other. I decided to make a digital album for each of us to remember the fabulous weekend. I loved surprising them by sending the albums out with a narrative typed account of our magical days together. As we have continued to gather each autumn, more albums evolved.

**Advantages of digital albums:**
- No printing necessary.
- Editing tools such as cropping are right at hand.
- Script can be easily added.
- More flair and artistry through colored pages and layouts.
- Faster completion of project.

**Advantages of handmade albums:**
- Knowing you touched them.
- Do not have to scan old prints, just use what you have.
- Add memorabilia.
- Others can help with the process.
- Additional pages can be added.

## Vacation or Holiday Photo Albums

Don't we take more photos during a vacation than any other time of year except holidays? For all the photos we take, how often do we go back and look at them again?

After a recent vacation, my smartphone suggested I view an album of the trip, which was automatically created for me, including music, by the program! Voila, all done unless you want to edit out all the duplicate or less than flattering photos. I did. A few more clicks and it could be printed and shipped to me, sans the music.

Would you enjoy having a holiday album? Of course, you would, but it seems so daunting to sort all those photos from past years. What if there were an exclusive photo album with only one page per year? It might be hard to choose just a handful of photos out of hundreds, but wouldn't that make the album more meaningful?

Thirty years ago, I had a brainstorming idea to make a Christmas album. It took time to go back and browse the photos in the old albums and shoeboxes to pull out the good ones. Funny, but a lot were of either duplicate shots or mediocre quality, so it wasn't as hard as I expected. It was a fun project and gets updated every year.

On Thanksgiving weekend, the album comes off the shelf and moves to the coffee table where it is on display until the Twelve Days of Christmas are over. I would love to do one for Thanksgiving and the Fourth of July, two other big holidays around here, but that has not yet happened.

## Framed Photos

Framed photos serve as an ongoing reminder of cherished people, places, or events in your lives.

Of course, unidentified framed photos tell no story if no one remembers the subjects in the pictures. One of my favorite antique shops holds a bin in the back of old family photos. It is beautiful, yet sad to see them there. I am so curious about the stories behind the pictures.

Outside of my bedroom hallway, about a dozen black-and-white framed photos of both my and Tom's family are displayed. Certain shots are over one hundred years ago. I can identify each one and assumed that everyone in my family could too. Not the case!

At one point my daughter pleaded with me, "Mom, you have to write the names on the back of the pictures. After you are gone, no one will know who they are." She was right, so I took them all down and identified them by writing on the back of the photo or with a sticky note on the back. I wish I were all caught up in identifying all the rest of my photos but have made a start.

## Special Collection Photos

Framed photos can also tell a story or highlight an event. Like my red dress series of photos which hang on the living room wall.

My mother was a saver, so I was not surprised when a little red velvet dress showed up when my oldest daughter was about two. "This was yours when you were her age," the accompanying note read. I had no memory of the dress.

Then a photo turned up of me wearing that dress with my little brother sharing the photo. I realized that my daughter was now around the same age as I was in that original photo. What if I got a picture of my daughter wearing the same dress? I made an appointment at a local studio. It came out beautifully.

Four years later, her little sister came along. Thankfully, I remembered the red dress before she outgrew it. I put her in the outfit and drove to the local department store where they had a studio. She was not happy about the whole ordeal, but I got the picture, albeit with tears in her eyes. I loved those photos and displayed each one for a time.

Twenty-three years later, my first grandchild was born, a girl. When she was about two, I remembered the dress. A photographer friend offered to take photos, and I presented them to her parents, my son, and his wife for Christmas.

Four years later they had another girl. Another round of red dress photos! Now there were four. Later that spring, I stopped by a garage sale and noticed two identical black frames with three slots for 5 x 7 pictures. I pictured those frames filled with red dress girls! I brought the frames home but still they sat there for about another year.

When I was ready, I started by taking the original picture of me and my brother to a shop to see if anyone could restore the old photo and edit him out. It was no problem for those technicians. Two weeks later I picked up the finished product and could hardly believe the high quality of the old photo which now contained only me in the now sixty-two-year-old little red velvet dress.

I gathered the six photos of myself, my two daughters and, by now, three granddaughters all taken in the same dress at the same age—two years old. Each one filled the slots in the frames and the result was stunning. Two more granddaughters later joined the family, so I bought another frame with three slots. The empty slot holds a photo of the dress itself. All the photos now hang on my living room wall and the dress is waiting for the next generation.

Do you have any classic items of clothing passed down through the generations? Maybe a christening gown, or special sweater? Can you find any photos of a relative wearing it? Even if you do not have anything now, you can start by taking a photo of an item of clothing you have now. You never know where it might hang later!

## Displayed Photos

No one played our old piano anymore, but it was an excellent shelf for family photos. The same ones perched there year after year like our family art gallery, while so many others languished in boxes.

I got tired of same old pictures on the piano all year long and decided to change them up. In my large family, each month holds at least one someone's birthday or anniversary, so that was a place to start a new collection. Many photos of loved ones never got displayed, so I decided to create a rotating monthly theme and put these framed photos on our piano.

If I have extra space, I will add a photo from a trip or significant event that happened in that month in the past. The piano is gone now, but a small table in the same spot holds the photos.

A friend displays old black-and-white photos in frames on her mantle which seems so artistic. I have old black-and-white photos but no standardized frames and no mantle. Still, the intention is there!

### Vintage Photos

It was a photo that started a family reunion one summer. One of my cousins found a 1925 family picture of my grandparents in front of an old farmhouse along with my grandfather's siblings and their families. Fourteen people in all. My grandparents looked so young!

Although all the folks in the photo have died, the house is still standing. In fact, I passed it often on visits to my mom. A group of us started to imagine how fun it would be to re-enact the photo. In the summer of 2018, sixty-four of the descendants of the original group gathered for a new picture after the owners of the home agreed it was a wonderful idea!

Cousins who I had never met showed up. We all chose a color-coded name tag from the original ancestor we descended from. One relative turned out to be a professional photographer, so he brought all the equipment. Afterward, we gathered for food and conversation and continued the next day with a picnic. It all started with a photo!

### Videos

When our kids were young, we did not own a video camera but rented one occasionally. An advantage to only have selective videos as we were more likely to watch them. I remember on the day my oldest was packing for college, we popped one of the old videos in a little TV on the kitchen table. All during the packing, the video played. My hope was that the reminders of who we were as a family would imprint deeply in this momentous time of launching the first one off.

### Slides

We also took slides of family vacations each year instead of pictures. When we got home, we could not wait to get the slides developed. Once we had them back, we would set up a big projector in the living room and relive the trip on the big screen. "Can we watch them again?" was the refrain. After we had multiple trip slides, we would watch one trip after another.

Later when they were teens, we brought all the slides along on a driving vacation to surprise the kids. Instead of watching movies, we watched slide shows of when they were all little—so much fun! I plan to transfer them to a digital file but am not sure if it would be as much fun. I don't know if anyone takes slides anymore but am sure glad that we did back in the day.

### Photo Gifts

Another use of photos is to give someone else back part of their story. One of my husband's aunts died young. All the photos of her ended up with her brother, my father-in-law. After his death, they went to us. For years they sat in a box until the mood hit to open the box. You know how that goes!

When I pulled out a lifetime of her photos, I knew they were not mine to keep. I tracked down her only son who lived in our area of the country and called to leave a message that we had the photos and could I send them. Two days later they arrived in his mailbox. I wish I could have recorded his phone message to me! He was blown away by getting to see photos of his mom and fill in her life story in a way he had never seen before. It was amazing!

Another friend suffered a house fire and lost everything including all her photos. My kids grew up with hers and I am compiling a pile of photos that include her kids, so she can at least have a little bit of her photo story back.

Another use of photos is for gift tags. With all the young children in our family I decided to use photos instead of gift tags for Christmas gifts. It makes the gifts easy to pass out by anyone. This is a great use for not-so-top-quality photos.

I have also started stuffing envelopes of photos for family and friends. Old Christmas photos are useful for this project. The recipients might not know what to do with them, but I am hoping these older photos might fill in parts of their story too. Have you ever received an old photo of yourself or a family member?

## Celebration Photos

School photos, first day of school photos, graduation photos, etc. can all tell a story. When our kids graduated from high school, I taped a photo from each year of elementary school and the previous high school years on the hall closet door. Of course, the transformation was amazing. It was fun to see the whole journey from kindergarten to college.

When my husband graduated with his PhD (at age sixty-eight), I turned again to my trusty Walgreens to make a congratulations banner, which featured all his previous graduations. The party guests all enjoyed seeing Tom at his grade school, high school, college, MA, and now PhD graduations.

It might take a little or a lot of time, but these photos are available somewhere and can be brought out to display for your next celebration event.

Our main goal in storytelling with photos is not to just pass on a box of unlabeled pictures to the next generation—like the beautiful wedding photo that came with the garage sale frame.

In the same way illustrations enhance a book, we fill out the life stories and events with actual faces and scenes.

We owe it to past generations, as well as future ones, to pass on as much of the story as we know with as many facets as we have. Are you ready to gather up your photos and start storytelling? You will only regret not doing it.

> Ask other relatives to help identify the family members who are mysteries to us. I do this through a Facebook group of my mom's paternal relatives. Posting a photo means a cousin can hopefully identify it.

## FAQ ABOUT STORYTELLING WITH PHOTOS

**Where is the best place to start?**
Whichever project is most exciting for you to finish.

**What if I only have a handful of old photos?**
Start with what you have. A simple album or display can tell a story. If you want to expand, ask other relatives about their collection. Photos are easily shared these days.

**My family does not seem that interested. Should I still do this?**
Yes. You can do this project for yourself. Very likely, someone in a future generation will value any story you tell through photos.

**Is there an easy way to delete photos on your phone?**
A simple way to stay on top of them is to put the current date in the photo search engine each day. All the phone photos you took on that date over the years will pop up. Delete all the ones

you don't care for. This takes a few minutes each day but isn't overwhelming.

## WHO ELSE IS STORYTELLING WITH PHOTOS?

"Years ago, I took a photo of a summer cottage that belonged to my friend's uncle. After he passed, I had a black-and-white enlargement made and hand colored it to resemble more of an old-time photo. The cottage was a treasured family gathering spot and I know the photo reminded her of one of her favorite places to go to as a kid and of one of her favorite uncles."

—Lisa Plefka Haskin, 61, Evanston,
Illinois, graphic designer/artist

———

"When I was a senior caregiver, the husband of a former client died. My husband took photos at the military funeral, and I made a wonderful book of the occasion using Shutterfly for her."

—Tammy Brown, 63, Chicago, Illinois, caregiver

———

"My albums are important because each page tells a story and brings back the memory of a special event in our lives. I organize them by year, with each book covering one year. Sometimes there are two for a year. I want to do wedding albums for my girls. After that, I will start by going backward and see how far I get. I want to leave a legacy of memories for our girls and hopefully for grandkids one day."

—Franci Henderson, 69, Hendersonville,
North Carolina, retired teacher

———

"Back in the day, I would put together a yearly photo album for my family, I have three brothers living, two have passed. Then another one for our daughter and her family. A few years ago, I realized that it made more sense to put the photos on a yearly thumb drive. I understood this when I counted over forty photo albums in storage boxes in my basement. Last year for our fiftieth anniversary I put together fifty photos in a yearly sequence and paid a media person to create a five-minute slideshow to the music of our lives. It was good fun for me and Meg as we recalled how we got to this juncture in our lives. I thought it was better to do it now, rather than wait until I am dead."

—William J. Dees, 73, Hannibal, Missouri, retired draftsman and high school teacher

### HOW ABOUT YOU?

1. Which photo stories do you most want to tell?
2. Can you identify your next step to make this happen?
3. Is there someone who can help you?
4. What would you most regret NOT doing with your photos?

# THREE

## Family Tradition Stories

### HOW DOES IT TELL OUR STORY?

Provides a template for celebrations
that are unique to our family.

### DEGREE OF DIFFICULTY?

Low to moderate, depending on the event.

### AMOUNT OF TIME?

Varied.

### COST?

Many traditions are free or at minimal
cost. Trips or tickets can be costly.

If you happen to be wandering by the shore of Lake Michigan in our town on the first day of spring, you might run into my husband and me. No, we are not out for a chilly beach stroll, although we sometimes enjoy that. On this day, we are picnicking, replete with sandwiches, deviled eggs, and lemonade. No need to worry about crowds for this holiday—we are always alone.

This fun albeit crazy tradition started on a warm first day of spring in 1975 in our young marriage. As I was getting ready to pick up my husband from work that day, I decided to take advantage of the beautiful weather and pack along dinner food in a wedding gift picnic basket to surprise him. We found an open table in a nearby park and laughed about how fun it was to have a picnic on the first day of spring. We have been doing it ever since. Most of the time it is freezing!

When our four kids were younger and tagged along, we went through phases like these:

"This is so fun to go on a picnic in the snow!"
"Mom, didn't you notice that it is raining?"
"This is *so* embarrassing. What if I run into someone I know?"
"Can I bring a friend? This is so cool!"
"Are you and Dad going on your picnic this year?"

Now it is just the two of us again, still picnicking. It is just what we do, our family legacy. On March 20, come rain, snow, blustery winds, or occasional mild temperatures, we still pack our basket to celebrate the first day of spring. Why? It is a tradition, one way we are known to our family.

Most of us have a handful of rituals and traditions that are part of our story and become our link to the past, enjoyment in the present, and hope for the future. Some of these come from our faith, our culture, our experiences, and others just seem to show up, like a balmy March 20 in 1975. I don't think we would have ever started this on a snowy equinox, but continuing it has never been in question.

You have these day-markers too. We all do, even if you have never identified them as such. "This is the way we always do it" shows up in a simple tradition of pizza every Saturday night, an annual Christmas Eve pageant, or a trip to Washington Island, Wisconsin, every September.

Whether they seem silly (like throwing a birthday party for the dog) or solemn (such as lighting candles for Advent), traditions define the identity of a family and are often passed down through generations. You might not have called your repeated celebrations or events "traditions." But if you have ever done the same thing more than once, you have the seedlings of a tradition.

How did these customs get started in the first place? Often no one knows, but there is almost always a story behind the scenes. Like our spring picnic.

Not all traditions start out spontaneously, but if you take a closer look at the roots of the traditions in your current family or your family of origin, they usually originate from four different sources, which are all part of your story.

## ORIGINS OF TRADITIONS

### Our Families

When we plan our celebrations, most of us start with the script of how our original family observed holidays, birthdays, and other important occasions. From the menu to the gifts to the guests, there is often an expectation of "this is the right way to do this" based on our childhood experiences. Of course, we assume everyone agrees with our assessment of "right."

This angle might lead to disagreements when you realize the same holiday can hold a variety of ways to celebrate. Often this shows up over the issue of when is the "correct" time to open Christmas gifts. So often, one family of origin opened gifts on Christmas Eve, while the other is steadfast that the only right time is Christmas morning! Has that happened in your family?

Even if you came from a family that had little celebration or traditions, you were probably influenced by something you read in a book or saw in a movie or on TV. Think about the traditions depicted by Charles Dickens in *The Christmas Carol*, the Halloween party from your favorite sitcom, the Thanksgiving feasts you remember from your family movie collection. Our impressions of how holidays should or could be celebrated are often formed early.

A new and innovative approach to major and minor holidays will develop over the years but we probably have a few starting components from our origins. Think about the way you celebrated the most recent holiday. See any similarities to your youth?

### Our Faith

Growing up in a liturgical church, the church services of Holy Week (the time between Palm Sunday and Easter) forever defined this solemn and celebrative season for me. The smell of incense can bring a flood of memories of kneeling during the reading of the Passion of Christ. The sight of lilies can trigger the scenes of the altar fully decorated on Easter morning. I still place a lily on my dining room table each year for this time of year.

For centuries, the church calendar has determined the date of some of the holidays we celebrate. Easter is based on a lunar calendar, which is why it shows up in some years in March, and others in April. The Jewish holidays are also determined by a different calendar than the one hanging on your kitchen wall.

I pull out our Advent wreath in late November to mark the four Sundays before Christmas, the Advent season that also begins the cycle of the church calendar. Some of my most beloved weeks of the year were brought to me by faith practices.

Of course, there is St. Patrick's Day on March 17, a day on which countless claim Irish heritage even if they're not! A holiday with definite origins on the church calendar even though it is more of a cultural celebration now. In all these holidays, stories of the faith help shape the stories of our lives.

## Our Culture

Most of us in the US stop the flow of the summer on the Fourth of July to celebrate with fun, family, and fireworks. In early July, my family hangs our giant flag on the garage, sits outside with our family and neighbors, and eats red, white, and blue waffles. Did I mention we also read the Declaration of Independence aloud around the table? When the kids got older, we stopped our annual "Fourth of July Quiz," because they all knew the answers.

Four months later, most of us spend the fourth Thursday in November eating nearly identical meals all across the country because it is just what Americans do on Thanksgiving Day. Canadians celebrate too, but on a different date!

I love these holidays when everyone can greet each other with "Happy Thanksgiving" or "Enjoy the Fourth" without worry of offense or the need to buy a gift. The culture gives us the holiday, and we celebrate it in our own fashion. The next generation observes and develops an ownership of our family rituals.

### Our Life Experience

Like our spring picnic, which few others celebrate in the same way, our life experience creates holidays out of our stories. "Gotcha Day" calls for a celebration to remind our family of an important adoption landmark day in December of 2019.

We celebrate the birthday of our home in January (more on that in Chapter 9). Certainly, family birthdays and anniversaries fall under this umbrella, but we all have unique anniversaries we might also celebrate that tell us part of our story. One friend always hosted a party to remember the anniversary of when her house caught fire but did not burn down. It was an annual opportunity to remember God's faithfulness.

Every Mother's Day for about fifteen years was called, "Garden-o-Rama" around here as my husband and adult kids pitched in to start the spring planting. As more of a fantasy gardener, I put off starting the process, thus the gift of the day.

Look at your calendar and see what you celebrate that might be unique to your family. All these rituals become our link to the past, enjoyment in the present, and hope that the specialness of family will carry on.

**Try these tips in your planning:**

- **Keep your plan simple.** Activities that focus on people and values are usually long-lasting. Despite their enjoyment, ideas that are too elaborate or expensive might have a short life span.
- **Talk to your spouse.** It's often the case that if your spouse's family spent lavishly on gifts, then your family specialized in stocking stuffers. If the in-laws opened

gifts on Christmas Eve, yours celebrated Christmas morning. So make a point of talking about which traditions you are going to keep from each family and what new ones you will start.

- **Involve your kids.** Children love to participate in something they have helped plan. They will probably have suggestions to offer about family fun as well as special celebrations.
- **Follow the same process** for all other holidays including birthdays, summer holidays, Valentine's, and even Halloween.

## THREE COMPONENTS OF A GOOD TRADITION

As you go about creating or revising family traditions to include them in the bigger picture of your family's story, consider keeping in mind three important components of a good tradition.

### 1. Chosen

The first component of a good tradition is that it needs to be *chosen*. I know, it seems kind of illogical. Don't you "just do it?" Why do you need to choose something you have always done? Sometimes a spontaneous event will repeat and might feel like a tradition but before labeling it as one, give it some thought.

Not all traditions from your family of origin will fit your current family. Even if they did, between keeping the traditions of both spouses, you would be overwhelmed with the "tradition of the day." Making intentional choices about which traditions to keep, which to drop, and which to revisit later is essential to maintain a meaningful set of rituals. These can be hard choices but will bring a great deal of relief in the long run as well as shape the brand of your family.

That time came for us after several years of running "The Christmas Marathon." Have you entered that race? The tagline is: "How much celebration can you cram into twenty-four hours?" Many of us run a few rounds of the marathon before we begin to wonder if there is an easier race. For our family, there was.

Before we had children, it was not hard to spend Christmas Eve at my in-laws', which was about a forty-minute drive away. But we wanted to see my parents too. So, we slept over at Tom's parents' home and rose early on Christmas morning for the six-hour drive to spend several days with my side of the family.

Then we realized we wanted our own time for Christmas celebration, just the two of us. We added December 23 as "our" Christmas, followed by December 24 with his family and the 25th with mine. Easy peasy!

Then we had kids. How hard can this be to keep up? Hard. By the time our second child came along, we were ready for a new plan. But which plan? Time to choose.

As a connoisseur of Christmas, I had stockpiled quite a collection of articles and books on how to celebrate this favorite holiday. I gathered them all up and headed off to a morning at my local library in mid-November and told my husband I was returning with a plan. And I did. What fun to create a template for the holidays that we are still using today, with some variations.

Interested in creating a new plan? Your plan will reflect your family and your personal values. Perhaps you love the Christmas

Marathon. It could be all your relatives are in the same town and it is harder to stay home, or you don't want to.

## 2. Enjoyed

The second component of a good tradition is that it needs to be *enjoyed*, especially if you hope it is passed down. This is simple. Have you endured traditions you just did not like?

Certain of my Swedish friends groan at mention of the appearance of the lutefisk, a traditional fish served at Christmas that to some tastes awful. It's not just the food! Do you really like staying up late on Christmas Eve putting toys together or rising at 5:00 a.m. to open Christmas gifts? Eating two Thanksgiving dinners to appease both families?

The same principle works with other holidays too. Does your family still enjoy apple picking? Pumpkin carving? Dyeing Easter eggs? Maybe. Watch for traditions to get outgrown, timed-out, or just not work anymore.

We had a decade or so of no Easter egg hunts. Now the grandchildren race all over the yard again just like their parents did. I could ignore Halloween for a time yet now I stock up on special treats for my neighbor's children as well as our own grands.

Now, to be sure, there are seasons where one or more of your children will not want to participate in anything. Mostly due to their age, à la teen years. In that case, hang on to a tradition if it is enjoyed by *most* who will participate in it.

A word of wisdom I heard about years ago from a mom of a large family was to plan things the older ones would enjoy and the younger ones will participate in. It does not work in reverse.

Before you ditch or modify a tradition, check and see if your perceptions are correct. Maybe your family likes the way you do something more than what they act like. It could be that the last time you didn't enjoy a tradition had more to do with whatever else was going on that day, not the ritual itself.

### 3. Flexible

The last component is that traditions need to be *flexible*. Some years, even the most beloved traditions will not work. Unforeseen or even predicted circumstances can alter even the most enjoyed traditions.

You always go to your brother's house for Easter weekend, but this year your husband has a new job and needs to work Saturdays. You plan a road trip for Thanksgiving and your car breaks down. Your child comes down with roseola the day before a planned trip. It will happen!

One year we planned to take the train to visit my parents on December 26. Our neighbor drove us to the train to save us from parking. We had no idea that the Chicago cold was so brutal that the train was cancelled. We couldn't just drive home. While we were scrambling for plan B, someone lifted my wallet out of my backpack. We got there but a spirit of flexibility was essential. The story lives on every year!

Other years included plumbing disasters, delayed flights, trips to the ER, and more. These events are all part of our family story too. Often aberrations are remembered longer than the times everything went according to script.

Only a handful of traditions survive the life span of a family. Even the best traditions can phase out. Circumstances such as kids away at college, a new marriage, a move, or death of a loved one can end traditions. Sometimes age pulls the plug as each child outgrows the activity.

The photographs, the videos, and the memories will linger long after the last homemade valentine is designed. No matter how long they last, traditions make us richer from having celebrated together.

**Traditions:** part of our legacy of days. Each one is a separate entity, but the composite of them forms a thick strand in the weaving of our story.

## FAQ ABOUT FAMILY TRADITIONS

**How do you know if a tradition is going to last?**
You usually don't until it does! This is how you know it has some longevity to it: if the tradition is looked forward to and talked about throughout the year.

**What if my spouse and I disagree about a tradition?**
Count on it! Try modifying your ideas until you both are ready to try it out. If a stalemate continues, try a "taking turns" approach. This works well in my house for New Year's Eve as we have very different ideas on how to celebrate. Now we take turns planning.

**Does everyone have to participate?**
Depends on the tradition and the occasion. I have a few traditions that are only mine as no one else ever shared the desire or interest to participate.

**Is it okay to stop?**
Sure! It is best not to make that decision in a moment of frustration, but step back and evaluate if a tradition has run its course.

## WHO ELSE IS OBSERVING TRADITIONS?

I asked friends to share their experiences with observing traditions, here is what they reported:

———

"We have a tradition of going to Cumberland Falls State Park the first weekend of November for the 'Unconventional Convention.' My husband is an amateur magician, and we go to magic shows as a family Friday night and Saturday night. He attends lectures and workshops during the day while the rest of us hike. When my son was little, he said that he planned to continue the tradition when he was grown and had a family of his own."

—Beth Peter O'Neill, 55, Lexington, Kentucky,
special education paraeducator

———

"My friend and I were both single moms with struggles with extended family over the holidays. We did pajama Christmas every year where we made pajamas for everyone out of the same fabric. We let the kids choose the food theme. One year we did breakfast Christmas. Other years were pizza, Southern, Chinese."

—Robin Meade, 59, Jacksonville, Florida,
IT project manager and writer

———

"We had birthday breakfast with dad. Mom was never a morning person. We'd get up and go early in the morning before school, just us and him. It wasn't always perfectly executed, but it was a sweet tradition associated with only Dad. He continues this now with his grandchildren."

—Maggie Vis, 47, Des Plaines, Illinois, graphic designer

———

"We have an annual Christmas sock contest. We keep our socks hidden under our pant legs until the judging begins. My ninety-one-year-old dad is the judge, and he chooses the most unique pair. We have a wooden traveling trophy that the current year's winner adds their name to. Everyone, even the men, participate. Homemade creativity is encouraged."

—Deborah L Ebenroth, 67, Bolingbrook, Illinois, retired

## HOW ABOUT YOU?

1. What is your most long-standing tradition?
2. What is your favorite tradition?
3. What tradition would you like to start?
4. Any traditions you would like to let go of? Why?

## FOUR

# Storytelling at the Stove: Passing on Legacies Via Recipes

### HOW DOES IT TELL OUR STORY?

Passing on favorite recipes or food traditions from generation to generation is part of a family legacy.

### DEGREE OF DIFFICULTY?

Depends on the occasion or recipe!

### AMOUNT OF TIME?

Some food traditions are quick, others might take most of a day to prepare.

### COST?

Ingredient expenses for recipes. Production costs for family cookbooks.

I sat at the salon waiting for my turn in the chair and picked up threads of the conversation going on at the station between my stylist and her current client. It was all about potato salad. Not just any potato salad, but *her* potato salad. A special recipe the stylist had made for her daughter's friends the night before, as it was a family favorite.

When it was my turn, I asked about the overheard conversation. "What is it about your potato salad that is special?"

"It's a recipe I got from my mom. Not, 'two cups of this, a couple tablespoons' of that but more of a 'feel' of how much to add. Potato salad is more about what you don't put in than what you do." I felt my hunger rising as she went on to describe her mom's spaghetti sauce. Another recipe from the heart, not a book.

Without realizing it, my stylist was telling me her family history with food at the centerpiece. An almost universal way of telling story.

Although many decades have passed, I can still picture the wooden picnic tables full of "covered dishes" at the local family reunions. Each large gathering only occurred about once a year, always in the summer, but with four branches of the family nearby, we seemed to spend a lot of Sundays hanging out with second cousins.

The main event was always the food, but we also gathered to catch up on the family news, toss around horseshoes, and usually share gossip. Fried chicken was a mainstay on the menu, and my mother got up early on reunion days to get hers going. Carefully dredging each piece in a pile of flour then nestling it into the popping shortening in her electric skillet. A skill, by the way, I did not inherit.

Coleslaw, which I was never fond of, was well-represented, and each of the ladies had her specially tweaked recipe for this picnic standard. A few pots of baked beans would be on the groaning table, and someone would dare to bring a Jell-O mold in the sizzling summer days. No worry about it melting because it was scarfed down.

The desserts were the stars of the show, however. Everyone knew that and waited. One of the favorites was Aunt Agnes's German chocolate cake. My mom never made German Chocolate Cake. No one else that I knew ever made it except Aunt Agnes. I can almost taste the sweet coconutty icing that dripped down the sides.

Besides Aunt Agnes's cake, there would be one of those chocolate cakes with the high stiff icing that took seven minutes to whip. My mom never made that kind either, took too long. Pies of every flavor invited the relatives to come and sample and we all did. Cookies and brownies also beckoned. Nothing seemed to come from a box. On a few occasions, someone brought along a hand-cranked ice cream maker and the men took turns cranking until the icy custard was ready to serve. Yum!

Certain foods can define a family for generations. The same standard offerings show up at the family reunions and are counted on to be there. Although family picnics like these with likely the same types of foods were going on in parks all over America, it still felt like "our" food. Part of our family story.

## HOW TO TELL YOUR STORY WITH FOOD

You might not realize you are storytelling by preparing and serving food, but this method of passing on our story to the next generation is the most universal of them all. All cultures, everywhere, cook and eat and, in doing so, pass on the history of their family by these ordinary tasks.

### Share "Early Taste" and Smell Stories

My few early memories of my paternal grandmother involved a drink: coffee! I was way too young to drink it, but she served it with huge helpings of sugar in her beautiful Fiesta mugs. That was the only time in my life that I liked coffee. I'm certain it was more than the taste but the feeling I had when I drank it with her: grown up, special, and a little daring.

I don't think my parents knew about the Saturday morning coffee. My grandchildren do as I have told them this story as I prepare cups of tea for them, my drink of choice.

You might already be strolling down memory lane remembering early tastes. Even though we eat around 90,000 meals in our lifetime, the early tastes are still so memorable.

How about food smell memories? Another of my early food memories involves a smell. The smooth sharp whiff of pimento cheese spread always meant we were going on a trip. The awkward food grinding contraption was attached on the side of the kitchen table and into it went the Velveeta cheese, jarred pimentos, and Miracle Whip. Out of it came a delicious spread we always traveled with. I don't recall having it any other time.

After my marriage, I found out you could buy pimento spread already made and tried it once, but it wasn't the same. My brothers and I still comment on our wonderful memories of eating those white bread sandwiches on picnic tables at rest stops across the country.

Most family gatherings involve at least one food that always shows up. What's yours? My family was quick to jump on the fondue craze in the sixties, and it became a staple at many celebration parties at our home. The basic Swiss cheese/wine melt with crusty bread chunks was simple to make with an impressive presentation. The guests came over expecting it, and my mom did not disappoint them. I asked for a fondue pot for a wedding present and received several but hardly used them and donated them. I couldn't bear to toss them as the memories of those gatherings were so sweet.

German chocolate cake, pimento cheese spread, fondue, and more. Foods, which were no doubt shared by many, but felt so unique to us. Every time they showed up, all the memories of all the other times our family gathered to nibble or feast were folded into the fare as well.

## Establish Food Traditions

Most families have holiday food traditions, but dig a little deeper and the weekly repeated meals are just as memorable for family stories. Was that how it was at your house?

Hamburgers were on the menu every Saturday night year-round for supper in my childhood and teen years. Mom would drag out the big electric skillet and fry them. In the summer, the grill was used when company was coming and then my dad would take over. At first it seemed boring, the same meal every week—then we began to look forward to those hamburgers. I'm sure we had side dishes, but I don't remember those.

When our first child came along, I remembered the simplicity of not having to decide what to make for dinner one night a week and decided we would do the same. But not hamburgers! Despite my mixed early memories of the pizza mix in a box (including the dry cheese), why not have pizza every Saturday night? I found an easy recipe for the dough and bought a jar of sauce and package of cheese and voila!

Hundreds of pizzas have emerged from our oven every Saturday night for over four decades with few exceptions, and it is still ongoing. The heyday of homemade pizza was the long period of the teen years with our four children when their friends would show up on Saturday nights to help assemble and then devour the many pizzas that those years called for. A common question we get asked is "Do you still have pizza on Saturday nights?" Somehow this simple menu became part of our family's identity.

Think about food traditions that were part of your past. Have you told your family about these? Recreating one of these might be a place to start.

**Your food traditions might include some of these:**
- Saturday breakfasts at the same restaurant
- Sunday night soup
- Wednesday morning chocolate chip pancakes
- Hot chocolate on the first day it snows
- Annual holiday baking days
- Ethnic food nights
- Ice cream on Thursday nights
- Annual canning and preserving

## REMEMBER NOSTALGIC FOOD STORIES

Mention TV dinners and the generation of kids growing up in the fifties and sixties will have a story to tell. Those amazing tin foil containers with the little compartments for turkey, mashed potatoes, vegetables, and a tiny spot for cranberry sauce were new to most American households.

We couldn't wait to try them! Our family enjoyed them on Sunday nights, the only night we didn't have to sit at the table for dinner. TV trays dotted around the living room, and we camped out in front of the television, watching the best TV night of the week with shows like *Bonanza* and *Ed Sullivan*. My brothers and I loved the novelty, and my parents appreciated the simplicity and negligible cleanup. A win-win.

Your family might not have been in on the TV dinner craze, but there was likely some new food trend they sampled and can tell you about. You also likely jumped on a new food craze. What story would you like to share about food trends?

**Have you told stories about these food trends?**
- Kraft Macaroni and Cheese
- Lunchables
- Hamburger Helper
- Rice-a-Roni
- Stove Top Stuffing
- Kool-Aid
- Grilled cheese and tomato soup
- Ramen noodles
- Hot Pockets

## Tell Funny Food Stories

Most of us have a memorable, usually humorous, food story which is passed down to the next generations.

One of my earliest hospitality dinner experiences involved researching recipes then preparing a lovely meal for two new friends from church. My young husband was taking an evening class, and I decided to invite them over for dinner while he was

gone. I was so excited to have my first guests and envisioned the
fun evening we would have. All went well until it was time to eat
when I realized I never turned the oven on! We still laugh about
that today, some fifty years after the fact.

Ask around at your next extended family gathering. Someone likely has one! I found out that one of my great aunts once
got the biggest ham out of the family smokehouse to fix for
her new boyfriend one Friday evening. Well, turns out the boyfriend was Catholic and at that time he couldn't eat meat on
Friday. She had forgotten about that!

### Rediscover Treasured Family Recipes

Perhaps I should have called this section "secret" family recipes,
as some of them indeed are! Is there a dog-eared recipe card
passed down in your family from one generation to the next?
Or a falling apart cookbook held together with rubber bands?
Perhaps a must-have dish on the Thanksgiving table that feels
unique to your family? Maybe an oral recipe like my hairstylist's
potato salad?

Family stories are laced with recipes. The Christmas season
isn't complete without the homemade Chex mix. A lamb cake is
always on the table at Easter. A jar of whipping cream is passed
around on Thanksgiving to be shaken until butter shows up.
Fourth of July means homemade waffles with red and blue ber-
ries along with a can of white whipping cream.

Famous fruit pies, legendary birthday cakes, the annual
Christmas stollen are some of the culinary stories that define
a family.

For our family, kolache is one of those foods. My husband's grandmother, known as Babi, emigrated to the U.S. from what is now the Czech Republic in 1901. I met her when I married into the family, and at the first dinner at her home she served a tray of her famous kolaches. Each one bursting with fillings of raspberry, apricot, prune, and poppy seed.

The plate was emptied, and we had to wait for our next visit to enjoy these delectable treats. When pressed for the recipe, Babi would shrug and say it was all in her head. When her health began to fail, she attempted to write the recipe for future generations. One infamous ingredient was a half of eggshell of water!

My sister-in-law reported that she tried again with a new recipe, and it still wasn't right. No one has able to make them like hers, but at any mention of kolache in the large family, stories of Babi's legendary ones are told again and again.

One unusual recipe from my childhood years was my mother's famous Mayonnaise Cake. For some, the name itself is quite a turnoff, but it is a delicious cake! The recipe came from the rationing days of World War II when both butter and eggs could be hard to come by, so the addition of mayonnaise took the place of those two basic ingredients.

Even though my mom had a high regard for cake mixes in a box, her mayonnaise cake was made from scratch and served for family birthdays. My brothers especially loved it and once we were adults and the brothers were in their own homes for their birthdays, Mom would make it for the Christmas visit. One of our sons was especially fond of the cake, so I was quite thrilled when his wife asked me for the recipe so she could make it for his birthday. The tradition continues.

### Mayonnaise Cake

Ingredients:

- 1 C chopped dates
- 1 tsp baking powder
- 1 C mayonnaise (NOT Miracle Whip)
- 1 C sugar
- 2 C flour
- 1 tsp cinnamon
- 3 TBL cocoa
- ½ tsp salt

Directions:

1. Preheat oven to 350 degrees.
2. Sprinkle 1 tsp baking powder over the dates.
3. Pour 1 C boiling water over the dates: Cool till tepid.
4. Whip 1 C mayo and 1 C sugar.
5. Mix the date mixture with the mayo mixture.
6. Add the flour, cinnamon, cocoa, and salt.
7. Mix all together till smooth.
8. Bake 25–30 minutes in 9X9 or 8X8 pan.

### Icing

Ingredients:

- 1 C brown sugar
- 5 TBL butter
- ⅓ C milk
- 1½ C powdered sugar

Directions:

1. Mix brown sugar and butter in pan on stove and bring to boil for three minutes. Stir constantly.

2. Add ⅓ C milk and scant salt and boil for five minutes. Keep stirring.

3. This is the tricky part: Add 1.5 C powdered sugar slowly while stirring fast so it doesn't harden. If you have another recipe for caramel frosting, you could try that instead.

### Locate Old Family Recipes

What if you heard about or remember an old family recipe but have never seen it in print? How can you bring it into your kitchen now?

One way is to ask relatives of the same branch of the family if they might have the recipe. I turn to the cousins' Facebook group to ask about and share recipes.

Another idea is to Google a recipe from a certain era such as "apple pie from the 1940s."

Old cookbooks are another useful source as well as websites like Lostrecipesfound.com.

### Create Family Cookbooks

This past Christmas I received in the mail a gift from a friend: her family's cookbook of holiday recipes. The author not only included the recipes, but photos and family anecdotes that came along with the food. What a delightful gift!

Another friend mentioned that her mom compiles favorite family recipes for weddings in the family. She reaches out to both the bride and groom's family and asks for handwritten recipes on cards and also asks to include a photo of themselves. She puts all these into a scrapbook for the new couple.

Some families have compiled a cookbook of favorite recipes contributed by various relatives and distributed around to different branches of the family tree. I'm not sure if our family has enough favorite recipes to qualify for such an attempt, but I admire those who do.

Family cookbooks can be as simple as a Word document or a sheaf of typed recipes stapled together. They can also be generated by computer programs or self-published and printed on Amazon.

Regardless of the method, family cookbooks hold much more than directions for how to make food but the bond of shared love and memories around a table.

### Teach Your Family Favorites

It's one thing to talk about family food stories, another to enjoy the food together, but to teach a younger relative to prepare the family favorites elevates the shared food story to the next level. Christmas often provides the opportunity for multi-generational baking or special food preparation.

My husband's Babi didn't teach me how to make her famous kolaches, but I did visit her to learn to make homemade chili sauce. She also created her own laundry soap, and she taught me that skill which involved saving a lot of bacon grease!

Who taught you how to cook a special recipe? Who do you wish had? Sometimes you don't know which recipes are going to stand the test of time and become part of the family lore. It may be the typical menu items that begin to create legends or the once-a-year specialties. It will likely not be your decision!

## FAQ ABOUT STORYTELLING AT THE STOVE

**What if you can't remember any food stories from your youth?**
Ask other relatives what they remember. One of my cousins reminded me of some of the family reunion food.

**What if there was nothing memorable about food to recreate?**
Start your own food stories. Create a "signature" dish or meal for events. If you prefer ordering out, stick with a theme for a certain gathering. "We always have Portillos at my in-laws'" was recently reported to me.

**What if you don't like to cook?**
I can relate! One of my favorite memories of my grandfather was watching him reach under the porch cabinet to pull out a "sodie" for me and my brother. No cooking involved but a definite food memory.

**I would like to create some food memories, but my family is so picky.**
Instead of guessing what they would like, ask them. "What is ONE thing to eat we can agree on?" and make that thing. Again, and again. Along, of course, with other items.

## WHO ELSE IS TELLING STORIES ABOUT FOOD?

"My mother was a pie maker. Whenever I make apple pie, I think of her. A specialty of hers was also fried pies. She sold them for ten cents each, and I would walk around the neighborhood and deliver them. She used the money to pay for building and furnishing her Sunday school room at our church. I got her to write down the recipe (she wasn't generally a recipe kind of cook, so that took some doing), and I make them only occasionally, as it's a two-day project. My family loves them and begs me to make them. Nothing brings back memories of my mom like rolling out the dough for each pie like I watched my mom do so many times."

—Ruth Madziarczyk, 73, Knoxville, Tennessee, homemaker

———

"My dad's side was German and came to the U.S. in the mid-1800s. His mother used to make a soup she called 'kuddle-muddle.' It had hunks of meat (not sure if it was pork or beef), cabbage, potatoes, carrots, and onion. I remember my dad made it when all his siblings and their spouses got together for a reunion, and they were all excited about it. I think it was a way to use leftovers. I don't make it myself, but I love the word."

—Meg Collins, 60, Chicago, Illinois, retired

———

"Family recipes are made for all holidays that hold special meaning to our family. My husband, Ted, makes the Schwartz dressing his family ate as a kid for Thanksgiving each year. He has taught our children how to make it as well, and they help make it each Thanksgiving.

My maternal grandmother, Bettye, gave me many of my favorite recipes for holiday dishes. Family traditions and memories make it all taste better as we celebrate. Over the years we've added some dishes that I hope my children look for in future holidays and always remember as they grow older."

—Sarah Schwartz, 45, Hull, Illinois, teacher

———

"I can't remember the specific Christmas morning in which my grandmother first made her now legendary Monkey Bread, but I was probably seven or eight. This recipe has remained a staple for every Christmas morning since. I can remember that first bite: pillowy, sweet, golden-brown dough seemingly made from the clouds at edge of heaven itself.

It's why we still make it in my house. Why my cousin still has a scanned picture of my grandma's original recipe card so she can make it every Christmas morning. Why our children all get so excited to shake up the raw dough in a plastic bag, just so each morsel can be covered in cinnamon sugar.

Who knew the power of this delightful pull-apart sweet bread could forever bring us all together? Or that we would all still make this today in kitchens stretching from Sacramento to Denver to Chicago to Tampa Bay? That the memory of sweet Christine could be immediately conjured by that remarkable scent and pillowy bite? Perhaps Grandma did."

—Joel Walker, 43, Evanston, Illinois,
executive creative director

## HOW ABOUT YOU?

1. What early food memories do you have? Where were you? Who else was there?
2. Is there a food from the past or a re-occurring meal you would like to revisit?
3. What funny food stories are told in your family?
4. If your family had a cookbook, which recipes would you like to see in it?

# FIVE

# Create a "Today in Our History" Almanac

---

### HOW DOES IT TELL OUR STORY?
Keeps track of the historical milestones within our family.

### DEGREE OF DIFFICULTY?
Medium-high to set up, low to maintain.

### AMOUNT OF TIME?
Two to three minutes per day to tell or about
ten minutes per week to send.

### COST?
None other than the minimal cost of the set-up supplies.

---

Like many families across the world, last Sunday our family gathered for dinner. But we didn't call it dinner, we called it a barbeque. And not everyone was there, just fifteen of us: my husband, Tom, me, three of our children, two of their spouses and eight grandchildren. The other five live in New Mexico and since we live in Illinois, is too long a commute for a Sunday afternoon meal. In fact, our entire family now gathers for dinner only once a year and those times usually include a Christmas tree.

For nearly a couple of decades, most days dinner was the one time we could count on a family gathering. Seemed like that daily ritual would go on forever. The eating part could flash by with four hungry children, so I was always looking for something to add to the sharing of the meal that the kids would enjoy participating in. Asking simple questions like, "How was your day" often resulted in mono-syllabic answers. What else could we talk about that would be fun and engaging?

Meanwhile, as a history buff of sorts, I always enjoyed the "What happened this day in history?" trivia question. Besides major holidays, some of the dates were easy to remember like Groundhog Day and St. Patrick's Day, but those only accounted for a few of the days of the year. Then I noticed our daily newspaper included this history feature each day called "Today's Almanac" which listed significant events for the given day. What if we enhanced our daily dinner conversations with the history of that day?

## Reviewing History

I can report that not all my "new great ideas" were successes, but this one seemed to work. Our family started an end-of-dinner ritual using the "Today in History" almanac in the daily newspaper as a conversation-starter. As the moderator, I made it into a nightly game. Not just revealing the info but inviting guesses.

For example:

Which city hosted the Olympics on this day in 1988? (Seoul,
  South Korea)
Who was president in 1948? (Harry S. Truman)
Who won the World Series two years ago?

The activity kept us in our chairs a little longer and we all
learned some things about events in the world. One spring morning as I tore off the daily calendar page, I noticed the date: April 9.
It seemed familiar. Somewhere between boiling the tea water and
making the toast, I remembered why. Six years earlier, April 9, was
the day we left on our big family trip to Maui for spring break.

Disclaimer: most of our previous spring breaks involved one
mandatory morning of extreme room cleaning (washing windows, vacuuming under the bed, taking books off bookshelves
and dusting, etc.) followed by pizza. Later in the week we might
go to a museum or the zoo, but we were a stay-home-for-spring-
break kind of family. Until that year. My husband's parents
owned a condo in Maui, Hawaii, and invited us to use it for the
week and included plane tickets in the offer. We jumped in with
our immediate *yes* and decided to add on an extra week.

The trip was amazing: snorkeling, biking, swimming in
beaches and pools and the unending supply of pineapples. We
all talked about it for months and were sure we would remember
every detail.

Now here it was six years later from the day we left, just an
ordinary Tuesday. I was curious to see if this day in our family's
history would stand out in any of our kids' memories. After we
did the "Today in History" activity that evening which included
Robert E. Lee's surrender that ended the Civil War, I asked if
anyone knew why today's date was important to us.

Everybody had a guess. Seventeen-year-old Jesh chimed in with "I started baseball!" Gabe, fifteen, thought it was the day he bought his vintage riding lawnmower. "People came for Easter!" added nine-year-old Christa. Selah, thirteen, finally got it right. "We went to Hawaii!"

The significance of the day was eventually remembered. Through our regular, "Today in History," facts and figures about dates and events that had nothing to do with us were now part of our table talk. But what about the events and anniversaries closest to our hearts? How could we acknowledge them as well?

### Reviewing *Our* History

Like all families, we have reached countless milestones along the way. In addition to the common causes of celebration—six birthdays, one anniversary, and assorted Hallmark holidays—there are dates for which no one will ever send us a card, but which nevertheless compose the fabric that makes us a family.

The day each of my children first crossed the monkey bars, the little league game winning home run, the time the basement flooded, the day our oldest child learned to drive. Like the "Today in History" items, these small events, taken individually, are just a list. Together, however, they define who we are, where we have been, and perhaps even suggest where we are going. I didn't want to lose them.

## FAMILY ALMANAC

The newspaper's daily feature gave me an idea: start our own "Today in OUR History" Almanac. But how to begin? I sat with that question and then a plan began to formulate.

The easiest place to start was to set up the project. I decided to use a card file system and purchased three hundred and sixty-six 3-by-5 cards—one for each day of the year plus the leap year day—and dated them. An oversized recipe box held the cards and monthly dividers. The system was in place but now the real work began.

The easy stuff—our birthdays, as well as those of close relatives, living and dead, were the first entries on the cards. No research involved. Next came weddings, baptisms, graduations, and deaths. Some dates were inscribed in my heart like the day we got engaged, others more elusive. I knew my university would know the date of graduation in 1972, even if I had forgotten! June 10.

Since the inspiration started with the Hawaii anniversary, I wanted to include the fun times we shared as a family. Some of the easier memories to record were family vacations. Despite many seasons of more "poorer" than "richer" we managed to get away every summer to somewhere, even if it was nearby.

## Vacations and Events

First, we listed the trips by years. My husband, Tom, and I had five to record before the kids were born and, of course, they did not remember the early ones when we packed up a car full of baby gear and headed down the highway.

So, the kids and I focused on the trips they *did* remember. One trip that kept us talking for a while was our adventure in 1988 to Walt Disney World. We planned and saved a long time for that trip.

"What do you all remember about that one?" I asked the crowd.

"Didn't we leave right after baseball season?" Jesh wondered. Gabe remembered our afternoon hike on the Appalachian trail during the drive down to Florida. Selah's memories were different: she was so sick at the theme park she had to go to the infirmary during the Electric Light parade. Christa was only two at the time, but she had heard so many stories about that trip that she chimed in too.

My husband recalled the week we left was the same time our beloved Chicago Cubs started using lights in the stadium for night games. We could all still remember the T-shirt "Let There Be Lights 8-8-88."

As a "selective" saver, I had a stash of hotel receipts and ticket stubs that were helpful for tracking the actual dates of other memorable events. That day after Christmas we saw *Les Misérables*, the time we went to the drive-in movie to see *Jurassic Park,* the overnight splurge at a local hotel so we could all go swimming. I could have told you, "We did this or that" but had no idea which year until I looked through the mementos or journals.

## Milestones and Memories

Some dates were harder to track. When did we get the dog? We remember the year, but Gabe recalled it was right before Thanksgiving because we wondered how the dog would do with a houseful of people coming over for the holiday. A check of vet records confirmed it as November 16, 1991.

On which December date did we call for friends and neighbors to help dig a deep hole in the front yard to save on labor costs before the plumber came? Looking through old photos narrowed that one down.

Medical events were another category. How old was Selah when she broke her collarbone in Wisconsin? Stepping back and looking at the other details of that fateful weekend we realized it was between fourth and fifth grade because her best friend, Kim, had not moved yet. Our kids all had chicken pox the same week. I had a tough time recalling what year that was. The pediatrician's office knew and provided the data for us.

The hardest dates to find were those for which no official record was noted. The day Christa learned to ride her bike, the first time we took a train ride, the afternoon Jesh beat me in our long-standing Uno tournament. Ever so much a part of our family record but never celebrated. Poring over my family life journal (see Chapter 1) filled in most of these details.

Sometimes photographs helped sort out the dates. A picture of Jesh's salsa-making venture shows October on the kitchen calendar in the photo's background. Gabe's first haircut included a vase of lilacs so that occurred in April or May. No leaves were left on the trees in the first photos of the sandbox Tom built so that was likely November. That narrows it down to a few weeks. More research of old calendars often clarified the exact date.

**What to Include in Your Family Almanac**
- Birth, Death, and Marriage Dates
- Graduations
- Military Service
- New Jobs/Promotions
- Vacations
- Acquisition of Pets
- Moves

- Major Purchases
- Funny Family Events
- Awards
- Major Weather Events
- Memorable Medical Events
- School Milestones
- Religious events
- Celebrations

## FILLING THE ALMANAC

At first our Family Almanac seemed so meager, many more blank than filled cards. But year by year, more lines keep getting added. Going back through personal planners and journals has been helpful, as well as listening to the kids' memories and then investigating the dates.

Like an archeological dig, I love finding old scraps of records and filling in the cards. Discovering my high school graduation program in my mom's basement was one of those finds. I couldn't wait to get home and add that event to May 19 for 1968.

For many years, the almanac became a standard part of our dinners together. Even if just a few of us were home, before we all split to homework, piano practice, the phone, or the dishes, we pulled out the day's card from the box. Not just for a conversation topic but to look at where we have been over the years: to remember, to guess, to laugh, and to enjoy our common identity. In all the years since we have been using it, events have become easier to remember. (Still, I update the almanac once a month with new events while our memories are fresh.)

One vivid memory is dropping off my then seventeen-year-old son on his first day at a new job. As he got out of the car, I told him he had just made the Family Almanac. His face lit up. True enough, we remember that moment every year on November 18. Watching him walk inside the building, I realized I do this as much for myself as I do for my kids.

To me, the almanac is much more than a collection of trivial days and events. It is a fossil record of the moments that have shaped and molded and defined who we are as a family. As such it is priceless and irreplaceable, and it is the first thing I would grab in a fire.

In no time at all, one child left home for college followed by the next and the next and the last. Sure, they stopped by for breaks and for the summer, but our family was not the same. Tom and I continued to check the almanac most evenings as we still dine at that same table where we all once clamored. Sometimes travel or a busy schedule resulted in week or more going by without picking it up, and I would catch up on what we missed. Always interesting, but my primary audience was missing. Years went by.

As time went on, sometimes a month would go by without a family history lesson. It nagged at me that I wanted to do more with it but could never figure out what would work. In what was probably a "shower thought" (you know how sometimes the best ideas come in that setting) a new way to share the almanac came to mind. I was excited to adopt it!

## After They Leave Home

Our adult children were in and out of our home but rarely around for dinner at the same time. Each had their own lives and schedules to keep as did we. I had emailed them from time to time with "Updates from Mom and Dad" to keep them up with what we were doing as well as hoping they might reciprocate with their own news.

As I am a girl who loves routines and rituals, I decided to streamline my updates to once a week, Monday, and called it aptly, "Moma's Monday Musings" even though I included news from Tom as well. This is a cheery note like, "we saw such and such movie, I am planning for a retreat next month, isn't it great the Cubs are winning?" stuff like that!

I ended the email by adding the line, "This is where we have been" and include a week's worth of history from the family almanac. By now I had made a digital almanac also, so it was easy to copy and paste.

Here is an example:

*Hi Loves,*

*The weekend was busy with two hospital chaplain shifts. The girls and I saw* Beauty and the Beast *Thursday night which was fabulous! I was at the hospital today for a few hours followed by coaching clients and then had women's group tonight and now I am thinking about packing for Phoenix.*

*We are planning an early annual spring picnic tomorrow before Dad leaves to teach at Trinity at 7:30 a.m. Are any of you planning to take a picnic?*

*Locals, please check in with Dad to make sure he hasn't drowned in his dissertation while I'm gone.*

*Much love, Moma*

Here is where we have been:

## March 18

1990 Little League try outs.

91 Selah had pneumonia.

94 Tom and girls visited the Museum of Science and Industry

10 Jesh and Jessica moved to Christiana St. YAY!! I took the kids to the zoo during the move.

12 80-degree weather

## March 19

02 Downtown with Selah

03 Iraq war started.

07 Started my chaplain job at Evanston.

11 Christa participated in a dance marathon.

14 I took Judah to Lutz's for an after-school outing.

20 Christa moved upstairs at the beginning of Covid.

## March 20

89 Six weeks of sickness

MANY years of Spring picnics: Warren Park, Hidden Park, Lighthouse Beach, etc.

20 Gov. Pritzker "Stay at Home" order (COVID).

## March 21

75 First ever spring picnic followed by all the others.

92 Eight inches of snow!

03 Christa went to Peoria for ETHS basketball game.

04 Dad in China visiting Gabe, Christa and I picnicked in the Rose Garden and ran races just like we did when she was a kid, and she won just like she always did.

14 Belated Birthday dinner for Jessica.

18 Personal retreat at Margarita Inn.

**March 22**

90 Broadway Review at Nichols.

96 ETHS family volleyball event.

03 Selah to Florida w/Mary Jo.

19 Judah to Quincy on the train.

**March 23**

71 Olive Schwartz, my maternal grandmother, died.

93 Jesh's first volleyball game at ETHS.

96 Selah to Colorado.

99 Kim K. visited; she and Selah went to a Bulls game.

03 Here it is boys . . . FIRST baseball fantasy draft!

07 Lou visited and we drove to Lake Geneva.

08 Easter with Bowkers, Omi and Stephanie also came.

15 Out with Selah and Camila to Lucky Platter.

20 First small group COVID Zoom for our family.

**March 24**

89 First of many visits to the Lincoln Park Conservatory.

94 Christa and I took Amtrak to Quincy.

18 Aaliyah and I took the train to Quincy. We watched *Gone with the Wind*

20 Tom started teaching his TIU class online.

Sometimes the feedback volleys back and forth like a ball across a net: "Oh, I remember that time," or a correction, "Mom, you got that year wrong" or a question, "What were we doing in Austin when our car broke down?" or a sibling interaction: "No, it was *you* who slid into me with your ice skates not the other way around." Occasionally, no one will comment at all, and I wonder if they even read it, but that does not deter me from posting again the following week. Sometimes if I am traveling or it is a busy holiday season, I will miss a week but I manage to string two weeks together the following week. It is a Monday ritual that is very dear to me.

Several Christmases ago, my youngest daughter gifted me with a calendar she created with a photo company. Each date listed a family highlight gleaned from the almanac. I was enthralled: she got it!

All four of our children and eleven grandchildren are already forming their own histories. Whether or not they choose to write them down will be their decision. I can only hope they do. But if they need a little inspiration, ours will always be here sitting here in the old recipe box on top of the china cabinet or in digital form in their inboxes.

Your family almanac is forming every day. Try keeping track of events on your wall calendar or using the "journal" app on newer phones. Any plan will work if you stick with it! Record now, organize later. Have fun with it!

## FAQ ABOUT THE "TODAY IN OUR HISTORY" ALMANAC.

**How is this different from the family journal?**
The family journal is comprised of the day-to-day happenings in the life of one family/individual. The family almanac is a compilation of dates which also include and honor individuals and events which occurred on specific dates before our lifetimes. Worldwide events which are remembered are included as well.

**Why do I want to keep track of all these details?**
The same reason historians track all the "this day in history" facts. To value these events and individuals who comprise our story. Our life experience is summed up in these memories.

**What if I do not have any records?**

Ask around to relatives and friends to see if anyone else has dates of events or relatives you share. Look at photos to see what you can identify. Check with public records. Facebook memories might help for more recent events.

**What if no one cares besides me?**

You caring is good enough! You are building this record for the future as well as now, and later someone else will care.

**Is there a modified version of this?**

Yes, you start with birthdays, anniversaries, and deaths and share those dates and go from there. Announcing "Today is your great-grandmother's birthday!" will start a conversation. Resources are available such as "Dates to Remember" books or download-ables to keep track of dates which could be a starting point.

**What about if I do not know the exact date?**

You could add a card at the end of the month "Other October Happenings" to include the events without a definite date.

## WHO ELSE IS KEEPING TRACK OF MEMORABLE DATES?

"For about ten years now, I have kept track of family milestones in a dated journal. It is one of my favorite practices, and it's so interesting to look back on and share with my family. It's fun to remember when certain events took place: When did we go to the Braves game last year? When did Zeke lose his first tooth? I also use a genealogy site for important dates for my ancestors."

—Susan O'Brien, 48, Acworth, Georgia,
spiritual director, homeschool mom, piano teacher

———

"I remember the date I started my job, the dates I bought and moved into my condo, the date I bought my most recent car. I comment about these memories to close friends, family, and coworkers, depending on who I see or talk to that day. Sometimes I will treat myself to something small—a book or some chocolate as a celebration. I have gone through a lot of changes over the past decade, so these events are a bit like 'birthdays' or renewal for me."

—Lisa Clark, 58, Lombard, Illinois,
lead customer service representative

———

"Besides celebrating the day my husband and I met, got engaged, and our anniversary, we also remember our oldest daughter's birthday and date of death and our grandson's birthday and date of death. We celebrate those by doing something kind for someone else and sharing their story as opportunity arises. Often on our birthdays or one of our anniversaries, we will find someone who needs encouragement or to go out to a fun event and we either take them out to eat or choose a gift."

—Delores Liesner, 80, Racine, Wisconsin, writer

## HOW ABOUT YOU?

1. Have you ever kept a record of the calendar dates of milestones?
2. What about the Family Almanac appeals to you?
3. Are you interested in beginning? What are some first steps you can take?
4. How would you like to see your date compilation used in your family?

# SIX

# Researching the Family Home and Neighborhood

---

### HOW DOES IT TELL OUR STORY?
Provides information and context for the places we live.

### DEGREE OF DIFFICULTY?
Low to moderate, depending on the depth of the research.

### AMOUNT OF TIME?
Varied.

### COST?
Minimal cost unless travel is involved.

---

"Why do we have a little door on our back porch?" was a common question during the "why" stages of parenting our four children. The 22 X 28 door that opens into the pantry has always been a source of fascination and the answer even more so.

I stood in the kitchen and attempted to explain. "A long time ago, the people who lived here didn't have refrigerators so that's where a big block of ice was delivered to keep the food cold. They put the ice in a box with their food, called the 'ice box.'" Although, I'm sure they couldn't fathom a pre-refrigerator home or picture a giant ice cube, the answer satisfied for a time.

As the children grew older new questions came up. "What is that skinny door behind the fridge for?" Show and tell on the spot occurred when we slid the refrigerator out to examine the space. Sure enough, the investigation revealed a pull-down ironing board that had probably been there since the house was built.

It is small and narrow with no padding, and I wondered how frequently it was used. Then I remembered in the era before permanent press, probably quite often. Since it was so hard to access, maybe the fridge wasn't always in front of it.

Thinking about other families living in our home and going to our pantry for their ice or ironing their clothing in my kitchen seemed fascinating, yet creepy. I pictured former residents looking out the same windows and noting the comings and goings of a different set of neighbors. Who were these people and what were they like? My interest rose and now that we started the conversation, the questions kept popping up.

"How old is our house?" started the next round of questions as we all began to realize the fact that our house had a history that didn't include us. Just like the children, I didn't know. I didn't spend much time thinking about the story of our house. Just keeping up with all the tasks involved in maintaining it was enough. Now my curiosity started to match theirs.

We all did agree that it was old! The frequency with which we blew electrical fuses informed us that our home was built well before the advent of air conditioners, computers, dishwashers, and other big electricity drainers. How much earlier? We realized that like other significant buildings, our home had a story to tell, and we wanted to hear it.

But how to begin to discover the lineage of our home was another question to answer. No packet of information came with the mortgage. There were no secret holes in the wall with a stash of info. No cornerstones with artifacts from the past. We were on our own.

## EVERY HOME HAS A STORY

Your home has a story to tell too. You might be just fine without ever knowing what it is but if you are curious at all, you can take a soft or deep dive into discovering the information. Perhaps you might not be interested in your current abode, but might be curious about the house you grew up in.

Research shows that Americans move at least once every five years. You might not be able to count all the places you have called home over the course of your life or like me, your moves might have been minimal. Whether you live in a single-family home, an apartment, condo building, or a houseboat, clues to the origin are available if you are willing to dig.

Exploring the history of your home or neighborhood might not seem relevant if you are planning to pack up soon, but for those who are interested in the story, it usually can be found, and you may run into some surprises.

This history of a home may not seem to matter, but a lot of the Old Testament has rich details about the exact layouts of buildings. God cares about where we live as well as the neighborhood. Acts 17:26 (ESV) indicates there is divine intention in place: *"And he made from one man every nation of mankind to live on all the face of the earth, having determined allotted periods and the boundaries of their dwelling place."*

My interest rose, and I was ready to take on the project to begin to research our current "dwelling place." It was time to jump in.

## GETTING STARTED

What would you like to know? When we decided to begin to research our home, the initial questions were easy: How old was the home? What was the original cost? What was the neighborhood like before the houses? And then, perhaps the most interesting question, who else has lived here?

Searching for the answers seemed daunting until I realized that like many towns, our city has a historical society that holds the local records: a lovely house near Lake Michigan that was once the residence of Vice President Charles Dawes. Like most local residents who don't frequent tourist attractions in their hometown, I had never visited ours.

Exploring the records in that museum seemed like a good place to begin. A quick call to check the hours was enough to move forward and plan the first information-gathering session. Even if they didn't have any answers, the staff might be able to direct us to another source. I scheduled a date.

Our youngest daughter, Christa, volunteered to help as it fit in nicely with a school project. Once Christa and I arrived at the "History Center," as it is called, we told the attendant we were seeking the story of our home. She immediately led the way.

"We have a file on most homes here in town. Let's see if we can find yours," she said. Within minutes, a bulging file with our address was delivered and was now open on the table in front of us. Our excitement was so high, and we hadn't even opened it yet.

## DISCOVERING THE RECORDS

The small cache of real estate photos in the folder first caught our attention. "Look at how small the tree is!" Christa referred to the now higher-than-the-house evergreen by our front door. In the photo taken in the early years of our home, it was about three feet high.

"Wow, the windows are so different," was my first observation as at one time there were four windows on the second floor where there are now two larger ones. Clearly some work had been done along the way.

"Wait, where is the garage?" we wondered. The backyard looked so long without it. Deeper in the file was the permit for the garage addition a few years later.

Our favorite find in the file was the building permit dated January 9, 1924. We decided to frame a copy of that for our front hallway. At the bottom of the permit, we gasped at the cost, $11,000. So much more to look at, but we were out of time for that day. We came home and filled in the rest of the family on our findings and planned our next research trip.

On our next visit, we retrieved the file again and reviewed the enclosed newspaper clippings. The first article that caught our attention was one on the architect. He was the same contractor who also designed a major office building in our downtown area, which still bears his name. We realized the similar homes we had seen around town were probably designed by him too. We began a pile of clippings to copy and kept on looking. Photos of previous owners and their noteworthy achievements were included. More fascinating for our baseball-loving family was an article that featured the story of the son of the then-owner who was called up to play for the New York Yankees. That news provided dinner conversation for several nights!

The attendant stopped by our table and asked us if we would like to know the ownership history of the building. What we had anticipated would take hours of research was easily available in city records, gathered in book form. Soon we knew not only who had owned our home, but also how long they lived there. We copied down those names for our project and mused about how strange it felt that other families had slept in our bedrooms, ate in our dining room, played in our backyard.

The last question we researched concerned the land. What was on this lot before our home was constructed? The area was once farmed but more interesting was the discovery that the land all around our neighborhood was once used for green-houses. That explained the few remaining greenhouses that were here when we moved in and what we had heard about termites in the area.

The home across the street had been converted from one of those small stores that were so common in earlier genera-tions. "Corner stores" were once very common in our neighbor-hood. There are none left now, although there were two when we moved in. Too bad that's gone for all the times we need milk! The elderly lady who lived next door to us and her husband used to be the shopkeepers in that store.

Christa and I brought home our copies of photos, deeds and clippings, and list of owners and put together a poster display of what we had found, and later I compiled all the records into a binder. We were proud of our work and wanted to share it with our family and neighbors.

## ADDITIONAL RESOURCES FOR RESEARCH

Researching a home is a lot like genealogy, following a trail. Besides local historical societies, other resources are available to help you dig. Depending on where you live, some of these might be easier to chase down than others, but with persistence you will be rewarded.

**Public Records:** Every county has an office of Recorder of Deeds although it might be called by a different name. There is a trove of information. Look for records in these county offices to get the names of former owners. Often there is a property file for each parcel. The newer ones are likely available online, whereas you might need to get physical copies of information for older buildings. Tax assessment records, deeds, or title searches can also be very helpful.

**Public Libraries:** Your local public library is much more than a collection of books. Many libraries also contain city and county records and can provide data on past owners. Consider calling a reference librarian in advance of your visit to discuss your search and allow enough time to browse the material.

**City Directories**: Published annually starting around 1800, these include a listing of residents, streets, businesses, organizations, or institutions. Although they are not still printed, past directories are a wealth of information on former owners and neighborhoods. Libraries and historical societies usually have a collection of these.

**Maps:** Houses built before 1960 are likely shown on a Sanborn Fire Insurance Company map. Starting around 1860, these maps were used by insurance companies such as Sanborn to assess fire risk. These maps are located at libraries, and I spotted some on eBay. A Google search is also a good place to start.

**Census Records:** The US Federal Census Records were taken every ten years starting in 1790. These are available and can provide information on who lived in a house, including hired help. There is a seventy-two-year access restriction and the most current year available is 1950.

**Subscriptions:** Newspapers.com offers a free trial subscription, which might be enough time to obtain information on your home. You can query your address or the names of former owners to see what turns up. **Note:** Not all newspapers are included in the data search, but I easily found the obituary of a former owner of our home.

**Findagrave.com:** Information on former owners from obituaries can be found at this site. If you know the names of previous owners, exploring a cemetery near a home you are researching might be rewarding.

## CONNECTING WITH FORMER OWNERS

It's one thing to wonder who else might have lived in your home, it's another to meet someone who spent time in your house. My husband and I were on staff at our church and often led small groups in our home for support or training. During one of these events, one of the men, Bob, remarked, "I spent a lot of time here when I was a boy."

We looked at him quizzically, "Here? In this house?"

"Yes, my grandparents owned it, and I was here all the time."

We got back to our agenda but knew we wanted to hear more about this story. During a break in the workshop, Bob told us about his Iranian grandparents, who were the first owners. I was interested to hear that whenever his grandmother needed a place to escape all the kids and the noise, she went down to the basement to the (former) coal bin. Bob told me that when she arrived at that small room, she threw her apron over her head to block out distractions and pray.

Hearing that was incredulous to me as I had recently claimed that same coal bin to use as a personal space to pray and work. Just like his grandmother, I was motivated by the desire to have a space away from the flow of the family with my own four kids. I didn't have an apron to throw over my head but found the same help in prayer.

Later, when I began researching for our twentieth anniversary in the house, I contacted Bob's widow, Karen, who provided me with more details and photos from that period as she was now the keeper of the family history.

## CONNECTING WITH NEIGHBORS

Another source is to ask neighbors who have been on the block for a long time if they remember past owners. I can still recall the names of everyone in my hometown neighborhood even though I haven't lived there for many decades. Sometimes all you need is one clue to get started.

Social media might help your research if you live in a small community. Often someone knows someone who knows someone or who might have an old photo for you.

### Prepare for the Next Owners

At some point you are likely to be the "former" resident. Meanwhile, you can start a file for future owners. This includes not only saving the historical information to pass along but creating a living history. Take plenty of photos of the outside and inside. Include a copy of the local newspaper. Also take photos of local businesses. In the forty-five years we have lived in this area, many storefronts have changed.

## COMPILING YOUR FINDINGS

Your findings can be compiled in a scrapbook or a binder to pass on to future generations. We also used a poster board to display the main facts for our larger family.

Since we started our house research project around the twenty-year mark of living in our home, we planned a party for the neighborhood to celebrate and share our findings from our research. We decided to invite everyone on both sides of our street even if we didn't know them and made a flyer to announce the date and time and went house by house to distribute them.

Instead of a meal, we chose an old-fashioned ice cream social theme and provided several flavors and an assortment of toppings. Over hot fudge sundaes we shared the results of our historical investigation and encouraged the neighbors to visit the history center and learn the story of their homes as well. It was a great party!

Even if you aren't interested in the origin of your home or neighborhood, one of your descendants might be. Can you start the trail for them or, better yet, invite them to sleuth with you? Your dwelling place is part of your story and any part of it that you share will be of benefit to those who come after.

## FAQ ABOUT RESEARCHING YOUR HOME AND NEIGHBORHOOD

**Where is the best place to start?**
Decide what you are most curious about: The age of your home, original cost, former owners, etc. and look for that first.

**Where is the easiest place to research?**
The local historical society/museum database.

**Why does this matter?**
If you are curious enough to do research, you might find interesting information about the origins of your home or neighborhood that your family or subsequent generations might appreciate. Knowing who else lived in your home is fascinating. Finding out the history of your neighborhood might provide data for current issues. Like my former greenhouse neighborhood encouraging termites now!

**How can I pass this information on to future owners?**
Compile a paper or electronic file with the available data and anecdotes. Provide this to the next owner and perhaps also provide the information to the local historical society.

## WHO ELSE IS RESEARCHING THEIR HOME?

"We live in the only brick house our area, an 1875 Italianate home which is made of cream city brick from Milwaukee. There were four fires in this logging town on the Fox river, and so it was easy to transport logs before the railroad was built. One of those fires burned some of the house. Then the owner decided to triple brick it since the foundation and much of the house was still intact. When the guy came to refinish our bedroom floor, he told us even more about the house and when each room was done because of the type of wood. Our local library and public museum were great sources of information."

—Carmen Leal, 70, Oshkosh, Wisconsin,
storyteller, Coconut's mom, reluctant gardener

———

"I know that our house has had just three owners in over one hundred years. The previous owners, the Duffys, owned a dry-cleaner, so when the people we bought it from moved in, there was no washer/dryer since all their clothes were professionally washed by their business. We have also been told that Mr. Duffy was either an alderman or had alderman friends and was able make sure that when overhead power lines went in, they did so on the other side of the street.

One other fun story: we searched online for information about our area and some videos came up with family home movies from one family that lived a few houses away on the other side of our block. The earliest shows the family playing in the snow in the early 1930s, and you can almost see our house, but not quite. It's fascinating!"

—Julia Moore, 51, Evanston, Illinois, higher education

———

"We bought our first and only home thirty-four years ago, and the tax description mentioned it being built around 1900. As we worked on renovations, we've discovered large beams that were more conducive to barn construction than housing timbers. I reached out to one of the former owners of our home, and the couple confirmed that the house had been used as part of the dairy farm that existed on our road. The enclosed front porch operated as an office, and the below-grade first floor (two steps down) housed the packaged milk.

We also went to our county assessor's office to find all the various owners and went to online census records to see who else lived here since several owners used it as rental property. We discovered a dairy farmer ran his business off our property. One day, a man who stopped by told us he was born in it in 1935. It turned out his dad worked for the factory next door!"

—Tracey Nielsen, 61, Grayslake, Illinois,
assistant youth librarian

———

"I live in a former country church and parsonage. Construction began in 1913 when church members scavenged timber for $60 from a sawmill slated for demolition. In the late 1950s, they built a tiny parsonage next to the church and added a cement tunnel and underground classrooms and bathrooms between the two buildings. The lower level is an adventuresome child's delight with nooks and crannies, a stone stairway that goes nowhere, and secret rooms—if they can tolerate a few cobwebs, some dampness, and possible critters.

I searched the web and connected with a former pastor who told me a little about the history over email. A local author published a township history book that featured several articles about the church that filled in details, and a sweet elderly woman had a scrapbook she loaned to us with photos of vacation Bible school and events at the church.

Over the years, people have stopped to take photos in front of the church, and we've invited them in for a walk-through. From PKs to former Sunday school teachers, they have shared snippets of their lives with us. The bell tower is long gone, and the pews too, but these walls have stories! According to the township history, a time capsule in the cornerstone contains a glass jar with a written history of the church from 1902–1913 inside. We can see the old stone via flashlight from the basement, but its secrets remain sealed."

—Michelle Rayburn, 55, New Auburn, Wisconsin, writer

## HOW ABOUT YOU?

1. Do you know any of the history of your current home?
2. Have any home research stories been passed down to you?
3. What would you most like to know about a place you've lived in?
4. What would you hope future generations will know about your home?

## SEVEN

# Fill in the Story: Interview Relatives

### HOW DOES IT TELL OUR STORY?

We are part of all the generations of our families. Hearing stories from the life of a relative in their own words informs us not only of the individual, but gives us clues about ourselves. In turn, we pass this record on to subsequent generations.

### DEGREE OF DIFFICULTY?

Most likely minimal.

### AMOUNT OF TIME?

The actual interview can be brief. Preparing questions and transcribing or copying the interview will take additional time.

### COST?

Minimal.

"You'd be proud of me; we interviewed my dad last weekend," my physiotherapist reported as she pummeled my back. She told me her dad was up in years and scheduled for a significant surgery. "He loved talking about himself and we learned so much!"

Finding out who and where we came from is a fascinating subject. Genealogy is hotter than ever as people seek the stories of their ancestors and spit into test tubes to ascertain their DNA. It has never been easier to locate the identities of those who have gone before us in the family line. Ancestry sites are popular, and libraries are well-equipped to handle the requests to know more.

I couldn't wait to open my DNA kit that I ordered for myself as a birthday gift. The older I get, the more intrigued I have become by those who have gone before me. A few years ago, I had plugged into a genealogy site and done some nosing around but was now curious about my own origins. This was my first experience with sending in a saliva sample, but I decided that was better than drawing blood.

While it is fun, and sometimes addictive, to dig for stories of deceased relatives, most of us have living relatives who can tell their personal histories without any research involved. Reaching out to older relatives to hear their narratives can be a family activity. Besides strengthening relationships, an audience for unheard stories will benefit both the teller and the listener.

In a family, folklores about relatives are often passed down. Each family has that cache of tales that always come up at gatherings. In our family, one of the famous ones is about the time my mom's dad drove his whole brood across the frozen Mississippi River in the 1930s to avoid a ten-cent bridge toll. That story never gets old!

While family legends are fun to talk about, it is even richer to have the stories told in the own words of those who experienced them. There are many ways to do this.

## WAYS TO GATHER THE STORIES

### Impromptu Recordings

Have you ever sat a phone recorder in the middle of a table to see what gets captured? At the time, it might seem quite random but might turn out to be a treasure. I have some old cassette recordings of my dad from one Christmas when he was reading a story. Nothing special about the story, but it is his voice that has long been silenced that is the real treasure. Of course, I need to research how to get it transcribed!

You might be in the middle of an event or even an ordinary day with your relative and the conversation becomes one you want to remember. Without breaking the flow, ask if it is okay for you to record the moment or take notes. Hopefully you'll get a yes and can capture the story. You often don't get much warning!

Look for opportunities that may be short-lived. During a time when my mom was recuperating from a fall and had a lot of time to sit around and rest, I decided to interview her with my phone. Not with preset questions but with stories I wanted to hear. I did ask her about the famous bridge story but also just asked her to talk about her life growing up. She had a lot to say! It was such a simple task but with huge long-lasting results. Soon she was back home and on the go again, and the opportunity was gone for now.

## Planned Interviews

While questions can be asked of relatives on the whim, scheduling a recording session ensures you will have the full focus and gives you a chance to think of what you might want to ask. Keep it casual. Try offering a cup of coffee or tea and keeping the tone conversational. Reassure your relative you just want to have fun with this.

When they realize this is a gift to you as well as future generations, they might be eager to help fill in the gaps.

It is common for one to think their story really is too ordinary. Sometimes it is the very story that "no one is interested in" that turns out to be the best of the bunch. Some questions you pose might result in short answers or an "I don't remember." So move on.

There might be a sensitive topic that your loved one has never spoken of before. In the twilight of their life, they might be ready to bring that up now. Don't push or prod but open the opportunity.

"Tell me more" can work, or a nod of your head. "What was that like?" can also open more doors. "I would like to hear more about that." Be sensitive but also on the watch for an opportunity to escort your relatives to a place to reveal a deeper part of themselves.

When your loved one seems to be getting tired, wrap it up for that session. You can resume at a better time.

Perhaps someone in your family has already done this. My brother and his wife recorded both of my parents in their sixties sitting in their favorite chairs in the living room answering questions. They planned for the interview in advance and prepared the questions they wanted to ask. To do this, they set up a video recorder on a tripod and jumped right in.

Those precious interviews sat on an old VHS tape for quite a while and then were transferred to a DVD. Now that is mostly obsolete as none of my children have DVD players, so they are currently on a thumb drive. Not too user-friendly for the next generation yet! It isn't enough to record but also to secure a way to pass them on.

If you are unsure what to ask in an interview, there are many resources on the web and in books to help you with guided questions. Sometimes, an open question like, "What do you want your descendants to know about you?" can open a lot.

**How to Pass the Stories On**

- Transcribe all non-written interviews and distribute within the family. Software is available to make this easier.
- Make multiple hard copies of any written stories.
- Create digital files of any video or other recordings.
- Designate several family members to be "keepers of the stories."
- Consider creating a printed book for multiple interviews to be passed down in the family.

## Written Interviews

We have all read countless interviews of famous people in articles in newspapers, magazines, newsletters, or on blog sites. Using the same type of questions as you might for an oral interview, you can capture your relative's story in a way that might be more easily distributed.

A written interview can start as an oral interview that is later transcribed. Another method would be to sit with a notepad and after asking the questions, write their responses. I also remember in the pre-digital era grabbing a nearby napkin to record some significant memories of my husband's grandfather that I was hearing for the first time!

---

**A Few Questions to Get Started**

1. Where did you grow up?
2. What was your school like?
3. What was your favorite subject?
4. Tell me about your friends.
5. What did you do for fun?
6. Did your family take trips?
7. Who were some other relatives you spent time with?
8. Did you go to church/synagogue/mosque?
9. How did you choose your profession?
10. What was the earliest news story you remember?

---

## Hire an Interviewer

Enlisting someone outside the family circle can sometimes engage your relative more than a more familiar person can. You might know someone in your circle who would be good at this task. Sometimes, however, hiring a professional interviewer is a good option. Keep in mind, this can be costly depending on the scope of the interview. An individual might arrange this for themselves to have a lasting legacy for their loved ones.

I once viewed a six-hour life story interview of someone I know well, which included video and still shots of places of significance in their earlier life, clips of favorite songs from adolescence, a survey of popular trends from their previous eras, and more. This was all in addition to detailed interviews which pulled out long stories of key events in their lives. It was the kind of documentary Ken Burns might have put together!

> **Take Advantage of Special Occasions**
>
> It is common to celebrate birthdays ending in five or zero for those in midlife and older. Why not use this occasion to ask some questions of the honoree? One person can be the emcee and field questions from the group. Another method might be to submit written questions for the birthday person to have a chance to think about them ahead of time.

## A FEW MORE METHODS TO GATHER STORIES

### Video Tributes

Video tributes are sometimes made after the death of a person to showcase their life. I have been to many funerals where I felt like I learned more about the deceased by what was shared at their funeral than I knew from real life. Why wait?

Each family has one or more tech-savvy members who can whip together a video full of photos and stories of an older loved one that can be shown before they are gone, like at a milestone birthday, anniversary, or family reunion.

In my family, we put together a video tribute for my mom's eightieth birthday which we also viewed at her eighty-fifth and ninetieth birthday celebrations and at her Memorial of Life Celebration. As we gather again this summer without her, we will view the video once again.

## Voicemails

How many of you have saved voicemails? I know I'm not the only one! My mom died in 2021 and I have five voicemails saved from her on my phone that are irreplaceable. I rarely listen to them but love knowing they are there. Most voicemails we receive can land in the trash, but if there are some you might want to hear again just for the voice, start saving them now.

Your interview of your relative might end up just for you or shared with current and future family members. Sometimes you don't know at the time! The end product may benefit the interviewee the most as they see the threads of their life put together in new ways. Give it a try!

## FAQ ABOUT INTERVIEWING RELATIVES

### What if the generation you want to interview are all dead?
Locate a living relative or close friend who had contact with the deceased. Ask them what they remember about your loved one.

### What if your relative doesn't want to be interviewed?
Reframe it as a conversation. The term "interview" might be intimidating. See if you can unpack their uncertainties. Are they afraid they will be "on stage" in some way? Go gently.

### What do you do with the interview?
Ask permission to share the contents with other family members by transcription or digitally. Ensure that it is in a format that can be easily passed on.

**What if you want to be interviewed and no one is asking?**
You can let it be known to your family that you would love to share more of your life story. Consider interviewing yourself! Write or record what you would like future generations to know.

## WHO ELSE IS INTERVIEWING RELATIVES?

"One Christmas Eve, my dad recorded a tape with everybody going around the room talking about Christmas, making jokes, and sending out Christmas greetings. Thirty years later, he found the tape. It was like Grandpa was sitting right there. As soon as I heard his voice, I remembered him and lots of things about him that otherwise, I would not have thought of because I was seven when my grandpa died.

Also, in eighth grade, my daughter chose to interview her grandfather about his time in the Army during World War II. He was married with two children when the war broke out. He wouldn't have been drafted but voluntarily wanted to fight for his country and enlisted. He rarely talked much about his time in Germany but had some souvenirs including Nazi arm bands. She wrote a paper and made a display of his memorabilia, pins, awards, and uniform and took it to a state contest. The paper and cassette tape are now at a local museum."

—Rebecca J. Cox, 68, Hannibal, Missouri, retired,
Sny Island Levee Drainage District/General Mills

———

"We gave my dad a book of questions, and rather than just answering them, he wrote a mini autobiography. It was a real lesson in existential perspective; funny how you can experience the same events and have entirely different perspectives. Or see some events as watershed, defining moments, and another person doesn't even mention them."

—Mike Gormaly, 61, Warsaw, Indiana, retired teacher

———

"During my years in broadcasting, I interviewed the head of the National Archives in Washington DC. He said to forget about all those family trees we work so hard to put together. Rather, sit down with your oldest relatives and ask them about their life. Get their stories. Stories are what matter. They tell us who we are and where we came from. So, I flew to Galesburg, Kansas, and interviewed my Grandma Gladys (my favorite relative and well into her nineties), with a tape recorder. The stories were amazing and were not only about her, but about her mother and grandmother and extended family. Things like relatives coming out west on a wagon train, being attacked by bandits, having all their possessions of value stolen, and being left for dead. But the women had sewn money into the petticoats of the little girls to serve as crinoline, so they still had money to continue on."

—Verla Wallace, 80, Ponte Vedra, Florida, retired journalist, author, and business executive

———

"In 1978, I interviewed my grandfather about their migration from the dust bowl to the West Coast in 1936. Their rickety Model A Ford carried three small children and was loaded with their few possessions remaining after the auction. They crossed the snowy Rockies on substandard roads in icy February. I wrote it as a college paper but kept it because even as recently as last month one of my children was asking for it so they could explain it to their children. The last of the family passed away last year. I still have the auction poster."

—Brian Chaplin, 67, Annandale, Virginia, retired

## *HOW ABOUT YOU?*

1. Which of your living relatives would you most like to interview?
2. What are you most curious to find out?
3. What is your next step to making this happen and in what ways can you make it the most comfortable environment for them to be interviewed?
4. How could this interview be preserved for future generations?

# EIGHT
## Traveling to the Past

---

### HOW DOES IT TELL OUR STORY?
Provides context and a visual piece of our history.

### DEGREE OF DIFFICULTY?
Minimal except for traveling.

### AMOUNT OF TIME?
A few hours to a multi-day trip.

### COST?
Travel expenses if needed.

---

"Let's drive by!" I can't remember which one of us said it this time, but my husband and I both knew what we were referring to: our first honeymoon apartment. It's usually a quick detour to view the old farmhouse in a nearby town. Our stay in that small place lasted only about a year but the memories feel lifelong. We are drawn back to our roots.

Some of us stay in the same area most of our lives with our relatives all around us. Look around at your next high school reunion and see how many still live in town. In certain parts of the world, that is still the norm but not in my circles. Staying put doesn't mean nothing changes, but the imprint is still familiar enough. Even if there are now different houses or stores along a thoroughfare, it feels like home.

Finding parts of your story, though, usually involves taking a trip. Even for those who settled down in their hometown, not every minute has been spent there. A segment of one's personal history might be scattered all over the city, the county, the country, the world. While photos can embellish a story, seeing the actual places can take it to a whole new level of detail.

Story-finding field trips to visit past family homes, jobs, schools, and cemeteries are fun and often revealing excursions. Even if the actual structures are no longer there, viewing the local area can be illuminating for you and your family. Often when you are "on-site," stories will emerge for the next generation.

## PLACES AND PEOPLE TO VISIT

### Visiting Previous Homes

Do you ever return to a place you lived in when you were younger and call all the houses by the names of the owners you remember? Even though we have moved, we seem to think those owners should still be in there looking just the same, right? Sometimes everything is as we remember like a frozen in time experience, and other times we don't recognize a thing.

Have you ever knocked on the door of a previous home and asked for a tour? What are you hoping to see? Stopping by homes we formerly lived in can tap into all kinds of memories. Details you might have forgotten show up crystal clear. Some realize their memory doesn't fit reality. That can be disarming. The house wasn't laid out as you remember. Often it is much smaller. Or perhaps it has been redecorated or redesigned.

For some, visiting a previous home can bring back or accentuate difficult memories. One individual reported, however, going back took the power out of the history as she realized how much Jesus had done for her.

My mother's last residence before her death was the same house we moved into when I was fifteen years old. Our family's previous home was just one block down the same street. Convenient for moving! During my frequent visits to her, I would stroll down the street to check out the home I lived in from ages two to fifteen.

One day, the current owner saw me staring at the house and asked me what I was doing. After I reported I spent thirteen years growing up there, he invited me in. What a treat to walk through all the rooms once again. For a moment it felt like home. It was a gift of great significance to me to get one more look.

## Tracking Down Relatives' Homes

My maternal grandparents lived on a farm less than a half an hour from my home. I spent many of my childhood weekends there sleeping over or visiting on Sunday afternoon with my family. I was so familiar with all the nooks and crannies of the old home that I could have given tours.

One of my favorite spots was the enclosed back porch where my grandpa would reach under the cupboard to pull out a "sodie" for my brothers and me. Those were a rare treat at my house. Likewise, the land all around the farm was equally imprinted. The "old house" on the property was more like a large storage shed. The coop was full of chickens that sometimes nipped at me when I gathered eggs. The rugged barn standing behind the pigsty, the white corn crib, the garden with the limp scarecrow, the spot where there was a well at one time were all forever fixed in my brain.

Nearly fifty years have passed since my last visit but even now I can call it up in exquisite detail. I loved to sleep over in my aunt's room. She was a teacher, and the room still held some schoolbooks and other interesting classroom supplies. I felt so grown up sleeping in her room. Did you have a place like that?

This grandmother died when I was twenty, and even though I came back to visit, it wasn't the same. Then I got married, so no more sleepovers either. After my grandfather died in 1976, I don't recall going inside the house as I no longer lived in the area.

All chance of ever returning was eradicated by the Mississippi River flood of 1993. The water took down not only the house and furnishings but all the farm buildings except one storage unit. No chance to ever go back now.

A few years ago, my husband and I drove into the property which is still farmed by my cousins. Nothing looked familiar except for one tree, an old cedar tree. As I stared at it, my cousin told me it was the same tree that always stood there. A single monument to all that once stood on the land.

If you have a place you want to revisit, don't wait until a flood wipes it out. There can be an expiration date for revisiting memories, but you don't know when that is.

Do you know where your older relatives lived? My mother-in-law, known as Babi to her many grandchildren, wrote her life story by typing it on her older typewriter where the "T" key always stuck. In her short memoir, she mentioned addresses of her previous homes and the names of schools she attended.

After her death, as we prepared for her memorial service, my husband and youngest daughter came up with the idea to offer a "Babi Tour" of all those meaningful addresses in her life. Her birthplace home has been torn down and is now a shopping area, so they did not include that. Fortunately, we had a chance to drive by years ago when the house still stood.

Before they invited other relatives to join in, some of our family did their own tours as all the other addresses in her story are still around. The experience was so meaningful for them to see each residence and school and imagine Geri as a young person full of life. The former pet store owned by Tom's father was also on the itinerary, although it is a different business now.

Instead of Geri's schools, which were not close by, we all drove by the high school where all her kids went. A stop on that tour was to drive by the house of famous gangster Al Capone who lived across the street.

## Checking Out Your Old Neighborhoods

You might be regularly passing through your old stomping grounds or circumstances involving your parents might offer you the chance to go back. At one point, my mom fell at home and spent rehab time in a local nursing facility. I took a train back to my hometown to visit her every week. The facility was right down the street from where I went to school and during her PT sessions, I would take a walk. It was quite a stroll down memory lane.

My first stop was my old school. The building was constructed during my kindergarten year and since it wasn't ready yet, for that first year I needed to go to another school which was also in the neighborhood. I only have one memory of kindergarten, but it was enough to pull up during that walk by the old, now unused building.

By the time first grade started, my school was ready enough to open but not quite finished, so we had some classes in the adjacent church. I remember being up in the choir loft learning how to read. It was fun to see the cornerstone for the school dated 1956. Yup, I was there then. The church right next door was also a very familiar place as we had daily Mass as part of our education. All my important church milestones took place in that church including my wedding.

Both the church and school now have different owners and I didn't get a chance to go in. The schoolyard brought up mixed feelings as I was never a good athlete and remembered my fear during a baseball game that I would have to catch a ball or not be able to hit it. Good thing I really like baseball now. Watching it, not playing.

I also strolled through the park my mom used to take me to as a child. It looked just the same. The first house I lived in until I was two years old was on that path too. I only have one memory from that home: the wallpaper! I took photos of every spot.

### Significant Places

Perhaps there is a faraway place that played a big role in your life. I wanted my children to see the exact spot where I started following Jesus when I was twenty years old. We didn't make a special trip there but a conference we were attending was nearby.

One afternoon during the week, we swung by the campus of Denver University where I attended one summer. More on that story in Chapter 10!

In the middle of campus is a chapel, Evans Chapel. Little did I know it at the time, but I would spend most of my life living in the town also founded by the same John Evans whom the chapel was named after. Can you understand why I wanted my kids to see it? We all piled into the car to head for the chapel. Places hold powerful history.

Ever go back to a camp from your youth? High above the spot where the Mississippi and Illinois Rivers meet is a camp in Pere Marquette State Park where I spent a week each summer with my family and church friends. Sitting around the campfires singing and engaging in deep conversations about life and God and many other topics seared this place on my heart.

Many years later Tom and I took a drive through this beautiful state park and found the camp. Of course, without the individuals who were so pivotal in my life that summer, it was just an empty camp. I'm glad that I got to show him the place where part of my heart came alive the summer I was seventeen.

### How to Preserve the Story of Places

- Invite your family to go with you to visit past homes/schools.
- Take photos of yourself/your family at every place you visit.
- Create a scrapbook or photo album detailing the places and the memories.
- Record addresses of significant locations from your past.

### Visiting Long-Lost Relatives

A trip to the past might be to see a person. Sally was my favorite cousin when I was growing up. Fifteen years older than I, she always seemed so beautiful and glamorous—not because of the way she dressed, but the way she carried herself. I guess you could say I had a cousin crush on her.

I was ten years old when Sally got married on June 25, which was also her twenty-fifth birthday. How perfect. I remember sitting in the church spellbound as she walked down the aisle in her beautiful white dress. I thought she was quite a princess.

I don't have any memories of seeing her after that as she and her new husband moved to Phoenix. I wondered about her from time to time, how was she doing. I heard through the family grapevine that she had four children in quick succession and then much later her husband died of cancer. I never thought I would see her again.

Fifty-three years later, my aging mom started talking about Sally and gave her a call. That conversation continued with several other calls and soon Sally sent me some old family photos that I had never seen. Not only did I want to see the photos, I wanted to see Sally!

My mom no longer traveled much but said she would be up for a trip to Phoenix. When we arrived at the airport for check in, she mentioned she forgot to bring her driver's license, so she had no ID to board the plane. I thought the whole thing might be off at that time but somehow, she managed to talk her way on to the plane and off we went!

From the time we met Sally at baggage and throughout our four-day visit it was like being at a long fun sleepover. Sally was as beautiful as ever. She pulled out all her family memorabilia, and we spent hours on the couch looking at photos and records.

Remembering for my mom, filling in the story for me. The days flew by.

I left with another cache of photos, many stories, and my own story was enriched multiple times by all the tales they told that were new to me. Twice a year, I return to see Sally since she lives just a few hours from one of my children. Each time I visit, more details emerge about my great grandparents, a great aunt I barely remember, and the famous farm where most of life took place in the thirties and forties. A treasure I could never imagine owning. I now also know Sally's children and their kids as the story keeps enlarging despite our fifty-three years of no communication.

My family has heard so much about Sally and seen many photos. My husband came along on one of my visits and it is my hope that others in my family can meet her too.

**Tracking Down Relatives**
- Ask relatives you know about the whereabouts of ones you are looking for.
- Try an internet search for a current address. Whitepages .com is helpful if you know their general location.
- Ancestry.com is helpful for family trees.
- Search on social media.

## Locating Old Cemeteries

Cemeteries are ideal spots finding out more about your heritage. On the twenty-eight-minute drive from Quincy, Illinois, to Hannibal, Missouri, home of Tom Sawyer, is a country road that goes up a hill. At the top of the hill is an old church, Bluff

Hall, built at the beginning of the Civil War in 1860. My ancestors worshipped there and are buried in the churchyard.

The first time I visited the churchyard to find the graves,
it took a while to locate them even though it is a small cemetery. Then, near the edge of the rows, I found them. My great-
grandparents, John and Laura Quintemeyer share a stone. Next
to them is the grave of their second child, an infant daughter,
Orpha Rose, who lived two months. In front of Orpha's grave is
the resting pace of their first child, Ida, who died at twelve years
old. A large photograph of Ida used to hang at the top of the
stairs in my grandparents' home. I'm sure it was carried away by
the Mississippi flood like the rest of the house.

My great aunt, Sophie, is buried there too. My only memory
of her is the day she died. Even though I was just four, I can still
bring back the call that my grandmother received announcing
her death. Scattered around the cemetery are more distant relatives, many of whom I knew when I was a child. Going there is
like a family reunion although all the attendees are dead.

A few years ago, I took my granddaughter to Bluff Hall for
the first time. It was a cold misty day, perfect cemetery weather!
As we stood over the graves, I told her there were her great-great-
great-great grandparents. She was impressed but I wished I had
more to tell her about them. Maybe someday she will go back
with her grandchildren and add a couple more "greats" to the
relationship.

Another churchyard that is near and dear to our family is St.
John's cemetery about an hour from our home. This churchyard
is attached to an old white clapboard church that held services
in Czech for my husband's ancestors. Story has it that Tom's
great-grandpa stood in for the priest and read the Gospel on
Sundays when the priest couldn't make it. The church is only

open once annually, on Labor Day, and one year we attended Mass in the yard and stepped inside. On the wall was a small plaque to honor our relative.

Each year, on the Friday after Thanksgiving, we drive there to pay our respects and remind our family of these relatives. Tom's parents are both buried there as well as his maternal grandparents and great-grandparents. Many great-aunts and uncles are nearby. When our kids were little, they used to play hide-and-seek between the tombstones. It might have seemed sacrilegious, but it was a familiar place to them from our annual visits.

Cemeteries, homes, former businesses, schools—all provide field trips to parts of our story which we still carry inside of us. What are we looking for when we go back? Parts of ourselves we lost track of along the way? A reawakening? Looking to fill in the narrative? Often, we find answers to questions we weren't even asking.

## FAQ ABOUT THE TRAVELING TO THE PAST

**What if I have no idea where to start first?**
Start with what you are most curious about. Your own past homes or schools? Your grandparents' towns or farms? Burial places of distant relatives? Take one excursion at a time unless they are all in the same area.

**How do you find out where your ancestors are buried?**
Ask relatives, usually someone knows. Genealogy sites often have that data as well if you look up your ancestor. https://www.findagrave.com/ has been helpful and often includes photos of grave markers.

**What if I can't find any buildings still standing?**
Visiting the area will still give you a sense of your own or your ancestor's past. Maybe there is still a structure that they might have visited like an old library or church. Local records should have some information or photos as discussed in the previous chapter.

## WHO ELSE IS GOING BACK?

"When my husband's, David's, parents were alive, we made a video tour of the places where they met and lived in Berkeley, California, which is also where we met and married during seminary. They also took us to places where my father-in-law's parents had lived (my in-laws and their parents all went to the University of California). We went back to the church where David's mom and dad married, and on the wall was the picture of the pastor who married them. They wound up telling us all about their wedding, as both sets of their parents were missionaries in other parts of the world and were not able to be at their wedding. The funny thing was that my hairdresser's place was across the street. Here I was, right next to the place where David's mom and dad had married! We have taken our sons back to Berkeley and also the house we lived in when they were little in Georgia. We also go by the house we lived in for ten years in Illinois whenever we go back to that area. That keeps the memories alive!"

—Rev. Mary Armstrong-Reiner, 64, McDonough,
Georgia, Lutheran minister/hospice chaplain

———

"I love visiting my old neighborhood. For me, the memories are happy; freedom, exploration, creativity, friendship, family, and security commingle. I can still feel the wind whipping my hair as I rode my bike (aqua, with a banana seat and sissy bar). The pack of neighborhood kids played hide-and-seek, freeze tag, and T.V. tag 'til the streetlights came on. We climbed trees, claimed best friends, ate blueberries, created mysteries, and came home to supper and a comfy bed. We moved before I turned into a teenager, which may explain the omnipresent glow of my vintage recollections. My childhood BFF Steph and I made a Quaker Road crawl a few years ago. The huge evergreens lining the property were the Christmas trees my dad had planted forty-plus years ago. There was the tree I walked smack into when I was pretending to be Helen Keller! There, the now-huge bushes that (gasp) I used to jump over!

How strange we must have seemed to anyone looking out the window as we walked back and forth in front of the house, pointing and snapping pictures. I decided to knock on the door to explain. A young woman answered, and I made my excuses. 'Hi, I just wanted to let you know that the reason I'm here taking pictures is because I grew up in this house.'

She replied, 'What was your last name?' I told her, and she said, 'Come on in!'

My kid brother, Johnny, had scrawled his first and last name on the attic rafters years ago. That was my ticket to revisit my childhood home. We walked into waves of memories: the shrunken living room (fondue parties, Burt Bacharach eight-tracks), the den (homemade carpet-sample rug, *Creature Feature* on Saturdays), and the backyard (what happened to the pool?). Everything was both familiar and strange. But the great gift of the day was this: the unexpected kindness of a stranger lent an added burnish to my memories of home."

—Melissa Ramer, Western North Carolina, writer, editor, translator

———

"I do travel back and almost always, the homes do not look as good as I remember, but I'm still drawn to do it. I've even been inside, years later, the house where I mostly grew up. Side note—I also feel drawn to go to places where my ancestors lived and breathed and worked, not just the cemeteries. I was able to stand on the approximate spot at Petersburg, Virginia, where a great-great-grandfather would have been during a Civil War battle and where his brother, who was in the same unit, died by friendly fire. Later this year, I'm going to the North Fork of Long Island to stand in places where some pre-Revolutionary War ancestors were."

—Melanie Rigney, 68, Arlington, Virginia, writer

———

"I found ancestors' graves while doing family tree research in the tiny town of Paoli, Wisconsin, and was surprised to learn that they had been key founders of Dane County, Wisconsin—the cemetery had a new marker for them put up by the local historical society. While I looked at it, a cemetery attendant asked if I had seen my ancestors' house. Turned out it was just across the road from the burial place. The current owners welcomed visitors and invited me in to see the house. It was amazing to walk through the home my great-grandmother grew up in. Most amazing—the style of house was very similar to the one I was living in then, in Northern Illinois."

—Debra Dimon Davis, 64, St. Petersburg, Florida, teacher

## HOW ABOUT YOU?

1. If you could go back in time, what would you most like to see?
2. What is the most fascinating thing you discovered in traveling to the past?
3. Which relative might have photos or stories to share with you to help you in your quest?
4. How would you like to use your findings to tell your story?

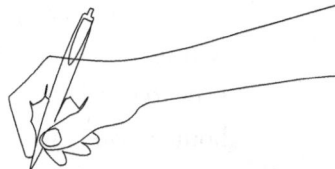

# NINE

# Writing and Reading Stories in Letters

### HOW DOES IT TELL OUR STORY?

Letters are a snapshot in time with details and narrative. They fill in gaps in our or someone else's story and can be passed on in original format.

### DEGREE OF DIFFICULTY?

Easy

### AMOUNT OF TIME?

Writing a letter can be a quick task. Finding old letters can take time, but the results are usually satisfying.

### COST?

Minimal. Postage and supplies.

The summer campers had already piled into their parents' cars to head home, and the group of us counselors gathered one more time to hand out awards to one another before we scattered back home to our various colleges. It was 1969 in eastern Massachusetts, the summer of the moon landing and Woodstock.

I was confident in my award and was waiting for it to be announced. No one else came close to winning. "And the winner for getting the most mail is: Tish!" A round of applause went up along with many comments about the quantity of letters that arrived for me all summer long. I wrote as many as I received that summer. My love for written correspondence continues to this day!

Letters are full of stories. Details of a day in the life of a writer, glimpses of the culture, stirrings of the heart, spiritual encouragement, heartbreak, and passion. Just like conversations. Unlike conversations, a letter can be revisited, tucked in a book, stuck under a pillow, placed in a box, and passed on to a new generation of readers in its original format.

As one of the ten ways to tell your story, a written missive offers a unique opportunity to be known to the next generation by your exact words in a small space that can live on long after you. Letters also provide unique perspective as they are generally written to only one person. The words convey not only the personality of the writer but also the reader.

Even though letters are written less frequently now, they have been around for thousands of years as the first known correspondence was written in around 500 BC by Queen Atossa of Persia. No one knows the content, but it set off the practice of personal written messages.

For previous generations, these epistles were the only form of communication to faraway friends and relatives. In war years, these were the lifeline for soldiers on both sides of the battle. A few letters from the Revolutionary War can be found on eBay for thousands of dollars. More correspondence from the Civil War years survives, which has been used in historical writings and documentaries.

Many families, including ours, have a collection of letters written during the two World Wars of the last century. More than any history book, these missives fill in the personal details of the day-to-day life of life of a soldier far away from home.

After World War II, the huge surge of the post began to dwindle as the survivors began to come home. Letter writing was still commonplace, but the presence of the telephone in most households began to replace written communication.

Emails began to replace letters as by 1997, about ten million users worldwide had free email accounts. While the emails could be printed out, as I did for a time, they were never the same as the personal touch of a letter knowing the writer had physically touched the paper.

## HOW TO TELL YOUR STORY WITH LETTERS

You might feel that the practice of sending personal mail belongs to another era, not too relevant to you now. However, storytelling through letters, both the ones you currently write and receive as well as ones you discover from the past, might delight and surprise you and turn out to be one of the best methods of preserving your story for generations to come.

### Pen Pals

Many baby boomers wrote their first letters to pen pals. The first pen pal service is believed to have been the Student Letter

Exchange which began in 1936. The organization's mission was to encourage students to learn about other countries by making new friends via letters. Pen pals could also be found through the long-ago personal ads in the newspapers and magazines.

Pen pals were promoted at my school in the 1960s, and I had at least three. Carol was from Chicago, about 300 miles away from my hometown. Her handwriting was very nice, and she used pale pink stationery. Her letters came faithfully about every week, and I learned all about her school and her family.

Another pen pal was Valerie who lived in upstate New York. Valerie wrote often and very long letters. I don't know if we would have been friends in real life, but our letters met a need we both had to be known. It was easy to share details of my life with someone who felt somewhat anonymous, yet caring.

My third pen pal, Mariko, lived in Kobe, Japan as my whole class had been assigned Japanese pen pals that year. This was not that long after World War II, so perhaps it was an opportunity created by teachers to bring more personal reconciliation.

I still have most of these letters from all three of my pen pals (see below), but I wish I had the ones I sent them to have a reminder of what my life was like in my pre-teen years. We held part of each other's story through those letters.

Pen pals are still in existence and a quick Google search can show you how to find them.

### Letters to Family and Friends

You might like to reach out to someone you know! Is there a relative you would like to be more in touch with? Writing a letter could be the first step in the reconnecting process. Maybe there was a cousin from your youth you no longer see on a regular basis, a faraway aunt or uncle, or a grandparent who would love to hear from you. Snippets of both of your lives can go back and forth on paper to fill out your stories.

When I was five years old, I met my California cousin, Robin, who is my age. My mom snapped many photos on that trip so when I came across them, I began to be curious about Robin. A few years ago, I found her on Facebook and reached out. We have still never been together again since we were five but have begun a correspondence that is starting to fill in the decades. It's fun to tell our families about their long-lost cousin who is now back on the radar!

Don't have an address? See if someone in the family does or try a Google search or whitepages.com.

How about writing a letter to a relative you do see often? Out of the blue, I received a letter from my oldest granddaughter when she was seven asking if I wanted to be her pen pal. This granddaughter did not live across the country but a mere twenty minutes away and I saw her often.

Of course, I sent a letter right back and we have continued the correspondence for eleven years now. She will be off to college soon so I'm glad we have this pattern already well established. Each of us writes things we don't say when we are together in the large family setting. It is a safe place to share our confidences, wonder out loud, and share life lessons.

I keep her letters in a special box in my office which is now overflowing, and I can't close the lid. Details of her life that I might not hear come across in the pages. It's fun to see her handwriting change over the years. We know much about each other through these letters and both treasure that.

## Embellish Your Cards

Everyone you know has a birthday once a year and that occasion can provide the opportunity to not just send a card, which is a great place to start, but to enclose a letter in the card. Do you have a special memory of that person? A funny story to recall? A detailed appreciation for their friendship? This might be more of a treasure than anything you could buy for them.

Some parents also write a letter to their child on their birthday sharing with them some of the highlights of the year and new hopes for the next year. A definite piece of a life story collection.

Enclosing a letter in a sympathy card can also be quite meaningful for the family. Share a memory, a special quality, or tell what you will miss. If you are really drawing a blank, Google "How to write a condolence letter" for help. I learned new insights about my mom after her death from the letters I received.

Some of us stay in touch with old friends through annual Christmas cards and letters. I must admit, I find it disappointing to receive a card without any personal touches, not even a signature. The ones I save are the ones that include a newsy note that really keeps the friendship growing. I try to respond with the same.

Many of us keep in touch with old friends over social media, but are we really sharing our story by a quick post or photo? Yes, that might be quite enough for many on our "friends" list but for those who are really friends off the internet, consider writing a letter about your actual real-life story. Even if it is not reciprocated, someday it might be.

## Find and Read Old Letters

I was a consummate letter writer in my late-elementary and teenage years. As mentioned, I always had pen pals of some sort and received many letters in return. I don't remember tossing them out but also didn't remember saving them either. Turns out, my mom did the saving.

In my mid-sixties, during one of our weekly phone calls, my mom mentioned she had been cleaning out stuff. Now she had been saying this for years and I usually just nodded although she couldn't see that from the phone. "I found some letters of yours," she reported.

My curiosity piqued. What letters? From whom? What kind of content? I knew I had to find out. My monthly visit to see her was coming up so I knew I would discover the answers soon enough. The closer I got to arriving on the train that day, the more intrigued I was.

"Mom, where are those letters?" I asked after what felt like a reasonable amount of time to be polite and greet. "Come on down," she replied and led the way to the basement. Sitting on the pool table was a large box stuffed with letters. My letters, to and from me. It was like a portal of time had just opened and I was back in the 1960s.

I pulled a few out and then realized I needed time and space to spread out and process this treasure. The suitcase I brought along was way too small, so I wedged a few in there and then drove to the post office for a couple of large flat rate mailing boxes and stuffed the rest in those and mailed them home to myself. My birthday was about a week away, so I decided to spend that day going through them. There were nearly a thousand, including greeting cards.

When the day arrived to start reading, I first gathered all the letters and categorized them. First by the ones I received and the ones I sent to my parents. Then by category of the sender: high school friend, camp friend, college friend, pen pals, random acquaintances. After that, I organized them by individual sender if I had more than five letters from one person. Greeting cards were in a different category.

I began to read them. I felt as though I entered a time machine and was back in my sixteen to twenty years, the time span of most of the letters. I remembered that version of myself but hadn't talked to her for a long time. It was like meeting an old friend!

More than the content of the letters, I learned more about myself than the writers by the way they wrote and spoke to me about our shared season of life. I recognized those aspects of me that were still my same authentic self and remembered parts of my persona that I lost track of.

I recognized I was glad to be rid of some of my previous ways of looking at the world and yet wanted to reclaim some of my early perspectives that I had shed too quickly. I sat on my bed all day going through the stacks. What a perfect birthday event! It was hard to come back to real life!

Quite a few of the found letters turned out to be letters from me to my parents from my first two years of college, including a summer I spent in the Boston area working as a counselor at a Boys and Girls Clubs of America camp. I found these stories of my coming-of-age life fascinating. I was surprised I shared details of boyfriends as I would have said I was rather private about that with them.

One letter that was meaningful was one I wrote the night of the moon landing, July 20, 1969, sharing all the details of watching it on a small black-and-white television that night at the camp in Massachusetts.

The famous-in-our-family, "I almost got arrested tonight" letter showed up too in reference to a Vietnam war protest I had participated in that resulted in some arrests. Not mine. The letter was a warning to my parents that they better tone me down so the next weekend, they showed up for a Mother's Day visit and soft confrontation of my extracurricular activities!

Reading old letters also gives glimpses of the culture of the day. One of the writers was the son of a friend of my dad from high school. We visited their family in California when I was a teenager and Ken and I decided to start writing letters. On my sixteenth birthday he sent me a telegram which was the best gift I received that year! We corresponded for about a year or so. When I reread his letters, he referred to not being safe to go out on the freeway. By now, I had no idea what he was talking about it. I Googled, "LA in 1965 summer" and read all about the Watts riots which were happening at that time. That was what he was talking about. Fascinating!

Other letters from the late sixties referred to Vietnam, current movies, pop music, and the minimum wage at the time. Reading about this era online is not the same as rereading a letter written in this era.

Finding the letters was an extraordinary gift and filled in chapters of my story that had slipped away.

## CORRESPONDENCE YOU MIGHT DISCOVER

### Family Letters

You might not be aware of a stash of letters from your past, but it is not unusual to run into old letters when cleaning out a home before a move or after a loved one's death. Soon, that may not be the case as less letters are written but at this time, it is still somewhat common.

War letters are often mentioned as turning up and for the first time, family members are hearing stories from their loved one's military years that were previously unknown. We have a stack of letters from World War I written by my husband's grandfather to his sweetheart (my husband's grandmother) that were found after his death. Beautiful penmanship and day-to-day details of a life in the service. Priceless.

Of all the letters in the stash my mother presented to me, the ones that meant the most for me were written by my maternal grandmother, Olive Schwartz. I didn't remember that she ever wrote to me. Sadly, at the time, I probably thought they were the most boring ones that arrived in my mailbox compared to the thrill of meeting new friends over ink, hearing updates from old friends, or possibly kindling a bit of a love interest. Now I treasure those letters and keep them in same box as my granddaughter's.

All the little details of life on the farm are so cherished, especially since I remember it all so well. Sometimes she would tuck in a dollar, which went a lot farther in those days. I hope I wrote her back. I'm sure she would have kept the letters, and they were probably lost in the Mississippi flood.

## Love Letters

Another type of letter that turns up is love letters. Probably because they were usually saved. For some, it might not feel appropriate to read one's love letters written to someone else in the family. Others find out details about one or both of their parents that help illumine their story in new revealing ways. Grandparents' love letters are fun as they describe the loved one known to us as an older, perhaps infirm, person as one young and vibrant and full of hopes and dreams.

I have a large cache of my husband's letters to me. Many of these letters were sent to me when I was serving on a mission team in Italy the summer before we married, and they would arrive in bundles as I moved around. Others were written during our engagement when we only saw each other about once a month. Aside from his then-handwriting being hard to decipher at times, his young love for me in his words is so tender to see. He also references places and events I have long forgotten and remembering them now is quite satisfying.

Do I want our children to read these after our deaths? Haven't decided!

### How to Make Writing a Letter a Pleasurable Experience
- Choose writing paper or a card that fits your personality.
- Stock up on writing utensils that you enjoy reaching for. Perhaps ink in your favorite colors.
- Set aside enough time not to be rushed.
- Go to a favorite spot in your home or café/coffee shop to write your letter.

- Play background music that goes with your mood.
- Purchase beautiful stamps either online or at the post office.
- Carry a few blank cards with you when traveling.
- Consider lovely postcards for shorter notes.

## HOW TO PRESERVE STORY THROUGH LETTERS

### Transcribe Letters

All the famous letters we know about in history are remembered and learned from because they were transcribed. Someone took the time to copy and preserve them for future generations.

A letter can be transcribed for easier reading, especially if the handwriting is hard to read, or copied in its original format. Letters which are copied or transcribed can be enjoyed by other family members. Permission is required if the writer or recipient is still living or by the estate if it is owned by someone other than you.

A transcribed letter can be passed around in the family by hand, by mail or email, copied into a notebook, or published into a book. I would love to have a record of my grandparents' correspondence, but none exists.

### Tell Stories About Letters

My mother wrote letters to her children on momentous occasions. She had much advice to pass on when I went to college and wrote it all down in a letter to me including her famous line, "K.Y.L.C." which she ended every letter to me with in my college years. "Keep your legs crossed."

My children have not read the actual letters (yet), but they know about my mom's postscript and life lessons she passed on in these missives. I have also shared with them some of my discoveries in the big stash of letters which they have found fascinating. The fact that these already-heard stories are recorded in the letters lends such credibility to them.

Another letter that is famous in my family that no one has seen is the "Dear John" letter my father received from his then-fiancée while he was serving in WWII. It was always a source of mystery that our dad planned to marry someone else. What would have happened to us? My brothers and I would wonder!

### Help Someone Write a Letter

Sometimes it is the very young or very old who need help writing letters and who have time on their hands to do so. Is there a child in your life who would like to dictate a letter for you to transcribe for them? Writing thank you notes is a good way to start this practice. They can tell you what they would like to say and then add a personal touch such as their printed name or a picture they drew.

At the other end of the life spectrum, perhaps there is an older person who might need help writing a letter due to illness or infirmity. At this point in life, there might be much to be said but not a way to do so without some assistance.

### Give Letters Back

Those of us who have a stash of letters written to us can give someone back part of their story. Letters belong to original author, not the recipient. That fact dashed my hopes for publishing some of the letters sent to me!

I created piles of letters belonging to friends of mine and began returning them, nearly fifty years after they were written. Some old friends were delighted to get this piece of history back and eagerly read them. Others preferred to keep the past in the past. One friend tossed them into a burning fireplace with no desire to revisit that era.

One of my college friends had specifically written in one of his letters, "save these for me" and I had! When I contacted him about sending them to him, I did not receive an answer.

Of course, if I didn't want to rekindle any sort of relationship, I did not offer to return letters. Old boyfriends were one of these categories.

One of my dear friends from high school was tragically murdered a few years after graduation. We hadn't stayed in close touch, but I still had a stack of her letters from when we were. I sent them to her sister as they contained sweet life details of her day-to-day life, like most of the rest of the letters, but a life that would end too soon.

In my current circle of friends is a woman whom I began to know first through letters before we met. Years later she was honored for her ministry at an event, and I was asked to say a few words. The most impactful words I shared were hers. Excerpts from the early letters where she expressed a longing to do the very things she was now being honored for.

Writing letters, reading old letters, sharing stories about letters, and helping someone compose a letter are all meaningful ways to share your story to the next generation. It is obviously one of my favorites!

Recently I had a seatmate on a long-distance train that was very chatty, in a kind way. While the country flew by the window, I learned all about her family and their comings and goings. Much more than she learned about mine! Her stop was before mine, but before she departed, she asked me for my address. Sure enough, I received a letter from her not long after the trip. And I wrote her back!

Before you write this method off as you don't think you have letters, ask around the family. Who knows what stack might be hiding out in a tucked away place. No luck? Then you can be the one to write the first one for your family.

## FAQ ON WRITING AND READING STORIES IN LETTERS

**What should I write about?**
The old letters that are the most interesting are usually the ones about the ordinary flow of life. My grandma's details about feeding the chickens or baking a cake are what I cherish. Share what you're doing, eating, planning, and feeling.

**No one writes me back, should I keep writing?**
Like cold calling, someone will likely answer eventually. If the practice feels valuable to you, keep it up and try different recipients.

**What should I do with an old letter I find?**
Read it! Share it with whomever might also be interested or have a connection to the writer.

**No one seems interested in the stash of old letters from my grandparents. Should I toss them?**
No. Attempt to find someone in the extended family who would be interested. Ideally, someone in a younger generation. If no one can be found, letters can be donated to archival repositories (www.archivists.org).

## WHO ELSE IS STORYTELLING WITH LETTERS?

"When I studied and traveled abroad in Israel, Tunisia, and Egypt, around Europe on a Eurail pass, and around Kenya, I wrote very long letters to my family and carbon-copied them into spiral notebooks. Last year, I read them and was amazed by how much I forgot, how unbelievably honest I was (my parents must have been terrified!), how funny I was, and how, beneath it all, I can recognize myself. I also kept all the letters I received from family and friends. When my father died, I found a box of letters he wrote home when he was in the army in WWII. I transcribed them all for my siblings."

—Valerie Hoffman, 70, Urbana, Illinois,
retired university professor

———

"My ninety-four-year-old dad and I write letters to each other approximately once a week. It's our way of communicating. We rarely talk on the phone. My heart still leaps when I see his familiar handwriting, almost always written with black fountain pen. He began writing to me regularly when I was a freshman in college, over thirty years ago!"

—Carol Pavlik, 49, Elmhurst, Illinois,
Lead Communications Specialist,
Elmhurst Public Library

———

"During the pandemic, I tackled several boxes of old family pictures and some from my dad in WWII. Little did we know that underneath a small layer of pictures was two years' worth of letters between my dad and mom during WWII. They were so sweet and tender, always comforting and encouraging each other: 'Made it across the pond. I don't really like big ships,' or 'Well you know, my love, about our big day a few weeks ago' (D-day). So hard to imagine your parents being so romantic! I treasure each one of them."

—Patricia Milazzo, Phoenix, Arizona, healthcare consultant

———

"Thirty-five years ago, I lost my mother to pancreatic cancer, three months before my wedding. Mother's Day was always very difficult for me until I became a mother. My mother was my dearest friend. When I was pregnant with my first son, I remember, as we were preparing the nursery, I discovered one of the dresser drawers would not close. It was my dresser from my childhood. When I pulled out the drawer, I discovered a stash of handwritten letters, written by my mother, tied together with a beautiful ribbon. Ironically, these letters were found on the second anniversary of my mother's death. Long story short, our son was born the day after finding this treasure—two weeks early. I felt my mother had a hand in having him born two weeks early and the day after the anniversary of her death. To this day, it's a day of the celebration of life, rather than a time to grieve."

—Annette Mota, 62, Skokie, Illinois, patient support assistant

### HOW ABOUT YOU?

1. When was the last time you wrote a letter?
2. Which letters do you wish you'd saved?
3. Would you rather own past letters you wrote or received?
4. Who could you ask in your family about old letters?

# TEN

## Telling Your Faith Story

In a small country churchyard in western Illinois are the graves of many of my maternal ancestors including my great-grandparents. The old red brick church was always locked when I stopped by to visit. My relatives spent many Sundays inside the church, and I was so curious about the story of the church and wondered what it looked like inside.

One winter's day when a larger group of my family stopped by, the door was wide open and the custodian invited us in to have a look. I sat in the seats and envisioned my relatives reading from some of the same Scriptures I read and singing some familiar hymns. It was a powerful experience but would have been even more powerful if they had left any record, oral or written, of what their faith was like.

How did they know God? What did they pray about? What happened with those prayers? Would their faith have informed mine? I can only speculate.

Each person of faith has a spiritual legacy of God's personalized activity in their lives. Biblical genealogy records indicate that telling our stories and knowing our place in the family line is important to God too. Whole chapters in the Old Testament and several sections in the New Testament offers long lists of family lineage. *"Let this be written for a future generation, that a people not yet created may praise the LORD"* (Psalm 102:18).

Joshua 4 includes detailed instruction about setting up a pile of stones to remember what God has done. Each family is tasked with setting up those stones for the next generations. Some of us have a large pile from the previous lineages to add to and others are starting a fresh pile of stones.

## WAYS TO TALK ABOUT FAITH

### Biblical Instruction

The Bible isn't at all ambiguous about the responsibility to pass on stories of faith to the next generations. Deuteronomy 6 and

Psalm 78 contain very clear instructions about how, where, and when to talk about faith. Psalm 78:1-7 offers some reasons to do the telling and what to include.

*"My people, hear my teaching; listen to the words of my mouth. I will open my mouth with a parable; I will utter hidden things, things from of old—things we have heard and known, things our ancestors have told us. We will not hide them from their descendants; we will tell the next generation the praiseworthy deeds of the LORD, his power, and the wonders he has done. He decreed statutes for Jacob and established the law in Israel, which he commanded our ancestors to teach their children, so the next generation would know them, even the children yet to be born, and they in turn would tell their children. Then they would put their trust in God and would not forget his deeds but would keep his commands."*

According to this psalm, telling your faith story to the next generation includes three things:

**The praiseworthy deeds of the Lord**. What are the deeds God has done in your life to bring Him praise? What would you tell if someone in your family asked for a story of how God showed up in your life?

**His power.** Kids love hearing about power, thus the popularity of superheroes. In your life, where is a story of God's power? Someone will want to hear it.

**The wonders He has done**. Tell them how you came to faith. Tell them amazing things God has done for you. Familiarize them with Bible stories through books, audios, and videos. Remind the next generation of their prayers that have been answered. Our "piled up stones" for future generations are "Remember when God . . ." stories.

Another very practical section of Scripture detailing the "how-to" of talking to our children about God's love is Deuteronomy 6:4-9.

> *"Hear, O Israel: The LORD our God, the LORD is one. Love the LORD your God with all your heart and with all your soul and with all your strength. These commandments that I give you today are to be on your hearts. Impress them on your children. Talk about them when you sit at home and when you walk along the road, when you lie down and when you get up. Tie them as symbols on your hands and bind them on your foreheads. Write them on the doorframes of your houses and on your gates."*

### Where to Tell Faith Stories

The passage provides very specific instructions for when to be ready to do the telling.

**When you sit at home.** Much of the "sitting at home" occurs at the table. While you don't want to script the whole dinner conversation, look for opportunities to tell a story. Was there a way God showed up in your life *today*? Is something about the season or the weather triggering a memory of God's intervention in the past? Some families incorporate reading or telling of Bible stories during or after dinner. Ask God how for ideas. Listen to the leading of the Holy Spirit. Watch out for trying to force something to happen.

**When you walk along the road.** You might not be doing much "walking along the road" but how about those captive car rides? Look for opportunities to talk about *"the wonders he has done"* (Ps. 78:4b) with your own voice or a creative rendering through audio stories of adventures of others who have seen God at work.

**When you lie down.** Right before bed or nap time is a rich opportunity to share a story about *"the praiseworthy deeds of the LORD"* (Ps. 78:4b). Sometimes the next generation wants to hear stories about when you were a child. Was there a time in your childhood when you were frightened and felt the reassuring presence of God? Did you ever lose something important to you and have it restored? Age-appropriate Bible stories are great for these times too but consider telling your own stories while you are putting your kids down.

**When you get up.** Maybe you are in the habit of spending time with God at the beginning of the day. Do your kids see you doing that? Have you told them why you set aside time to pray/journal/read? Can they join you in some way without taking too much away from your time?

**Write them on the doorframes of your house.** In the area where we live, it is common to see a little compartment, called a Mezuzah, which contains a tiny rolled up document of the Ten Commandments posted on the door frames. I'm not sure exactly what that part of the passage means for those of us who are not Jewish but have a few ideas. When you walk into someone's home, it is not hard to pick up a sense of what is important to the family by looking at what is on the walls.

Years ago, I read a story about a family where three of the sons followed a career centered in water. Neither of the parents were the "water sort." They didn't have a family boat or a vacation home on the water. One thing that they did have was a piece of art hanging in the dining room that featured men at sea. Perhaps that was imprinted on their hearts at each meal.

When I read that story, I ran out that day to buy a large print of a picture of Jesus holding a child and put it on a bedroom wall. Books on the shelf, music in the air, and art on the wall can all spread the *fragrance of Christ* (2 Cor. 2:14, ESV).

---

**Ideas for Telling Faith Stories**
- An encounter with God you had when you were a child.
- A specific answer to prayer.
- A miracle story you heard or read about.
- Something you thought you heard God say to you.
- The time you felt closest to God.
- A time you felt forgiven.
- The strongest belief you have about God.
- How your relationship with God started.
- Your baptism or other sacrament.

---

## PRACTICAL TIPS FOR TELLING YOUR FAITH STORY

### Prepare in Prayer

The Bible reminds us often to remember what He has done and tell the next generation. *"Only be careful, and watch yourselves closely so that you do not forget the things your eyes have seen or let them fade from your heart as long as you live. Teach them to your children and to their children after them"* (Deuteronomy 4:9).

Do you have stories of God's power? His faithfulness? His provision? Great things He has done in your family? If you are drawing somewhat of a blank, ask God to stir up those memories.

Psalm 145:4-7 also includes a similar theme.

*"One generation commends your works to another; they tell of your mighty acts. They speak of the glorious splendor of your majesty—and I will meditate on your wonderful works. They tell of the power of your awesome works—and I will proclaim your great deeds. They celebrate your abundant goodness and joyfully sing of your righteousness.*

Pray for open ears and hearts of the next generation, teachable moments, and good timing. Have you noticed how most of our significant interactions with our children seem to happen spontaneously? But we can prepare in prayer.

## Make a Written Account

The Gospel of Luke starts out by explaining the purpose of the writing of the Gospel was to compile an orderly written account. What if the stories of God showing up in your life were written in story form? Some of you may undertake that project to have a record for yourself and later for your family. Don't panic! You don't have to write a book, unless you want to! A hand-written or electronic document is a good place to start. Later you can decide how to use this.

Whether you eventually write them or not, you can begin telling them to the next generation. Psalm 111:4a says, *"He has caused his wonders to be remembered"* and your stories of God's work in your life are part of that chain of remembrances.

## Tell Family Stories about God

I was very close to my paternal grandmother and spent a lot of time in her home. She died when I was eleven, so all my memories stop there, but that was enough time to impart much to me. I rarely remember her talking to me about spiritual things, but one story she told me left a huge impact.

Grandma had some sort of surgery in which she had a complication. I remember none of those details. Her husband, my grandfather, died suddenly just after I turned three. She reported to me that at the time of this medical crisis, she had a near-death experience. She didn't call it that, but I knew that's what it was. She said she was in a tunnel of sorts with a light beckoning her. She was given the choice to move toward her deceased husband or to move toward me. Life or death. What did she want? She chose me.

Her sharing that story, while she didn't get all religious about it, has always been so reassuring to me. When someone you love has an experience of God's presence in a remarkable way and shares that with you, it can be very formative.

In those few years we had together after this experience, she taught me, by her example, how to be a wonderful grandmother. I now use those skills all the time with my current eleven grandchildren and replicate her style in many areas.

### Discuss Supernatural Events

My beloved mother-in-law was a deeply spiritual woman, which everyone knew, although she wasn't big on talking about it all the time. One year for Christmas, she presented us with a written story of her life which everyone loved. In that compilation of memories, she told two stories of what she believed were angelic interventions when she was at a point of danger. She will never be able to convey those stories directly to the next generations, but we have a written record of them, and each family has a copy.

When I was twenty years old and had been following Jesus for about a month, I also had an encounter with what I believe was an angel. I ran out of gas in a borrowed car on a busy highway in rush hour in an unfamiliar city. Suddenly, a man carrying a gas can approached the car and filled it without saying a word. I have shared that story with my children and am now including it in an anthology of stories for my grandchildren of amazing things God has done for me.

### Stick to the Facts

When you tell your story, don't try to interpret it. Just tell what happened. "The wonders he has done," "The power of his awesome works," etc. Let the Holy Spirit do the interpretation. That story may get filed in a child's memory and pulled out much later to reflect on.

As each family has stories of the time . . . *the car crashed into our house on Christmas; our daughter got sick at Disney World and spent the rest of the time in a wheelchair there; Dad jacked the house up for a repair; the kid that played soccer on the roof and then needed to go to the ER for stitches after colliding with a window; the time our house was broken into.*

The ones you tell repeatedly when you get together. Are there stories of God's intervention or a special gift that can only be attributed to Him that can be included in those stories? Maybe not so far, but be on the lookout.

This doesn't have to be a recent story. Don't think because nothing extraordinary seemed to happen today, there is nothing to tell. The stories in the Bible are millenniums old and are still being told. I recently had an occasion to recount the story in 2 Kings 6 about the borrowed axe that fell in the water and Elisha threw a stick in to make it float so it could be retrieved. Such a "small" miracle, yet it's right in the book along with all the other stories of God's power. That story fit into the situation that was playing out that day in my home.

## HOW TO TELL YOUR FAITH STORY

Sometimes we don't tell a story because we have no idea how to do that. I discovered a simple way to tell your own story of encountering God or something He did for you.

Here is the format for my conversion experience.

**When did it happen?** I was twenty years old.

**Where did it happen?** On the campus of Denver University outside Evans Chapel.

**Who was involved?** Me and a twenty-something guy who was passing out tracts on campus.

**What happened?** I had been going to this chapel for several evenings and laying on the floor (when I was alone) to cry out to God whom I wasn't sure was there. One evening as I came out, this guy handed me a tract called "The Permanent Revolution," which reflected the cultural times. I told him I wasn't interested in religion, and he told me it was about following Jesus, not a church. He asked me to find a Bible and read the Gospel of John. That was it. We did not exchange names or phone numbers.

**What action did I take to follow God?** I asked my roommate if she had a Bible and began to read. Later, someone from that group called my other roommate and asked her to go to a Bible study. She declined, but I got on the phone and said I was interested. I went to the study and about a month later committed my life to following Jesus.

**What benefit did I receive from God?** I have followed Him since that time. I now live in the town founded by the same man who founded the university and named the chapel after himself.

The formula works for almost any story. Similar to the newspaper article—who, what, when, where, why, how.

We have no idea what ripple effect one story might have. I have already told the story of my grandmother's near-death experience to some of my grandchildren, four generations after her. We don't know which ones will stick and which will be forgotten, but that's not our responsibility.

*"I will give you thanks in the great assembly; among the throngs I will praise you"* (Psalm 35:18). Could this "great assembly" include multi-generations of our family? If not you, then who will tell of the wonders He has done for you?

## FAQ ON TELLING YOUR FAITH STORY

**What if you're uncomfortable talking about spiritual experiences?**
Keep in mind the "this is what happened" theme without trying to include a sermon. Consider writing your stories down for a future time.

**What if no one seems interested?**
You are not responsible for how any story is received. Haven't we all heard stories or info that seemed irrelevant until a later point when it did?

**What if you are no longer practicing the faith of your earlier life?**
You may have changed your theology, but the stories remain.

**What if you're not sure about your spiritual experience?**
Say that. "I'm not sure how to explain this but this is what happened."

## WHO ELSE HEARD FAITH STORIES?

"I learned from watching the older saints, many who endured WWII in Europe but had a zest for life and a deep faith that they lived daily. No need for many words."

—Cleo Lampos, 78, Oak Lawn, Illinois,
chaplain, retired schoolteacher

———

"I was taught by relatives who helped me to identify areas of strength and areas of growth needed. They invited me into prayer regarding questions and situations. Prayed over me. Sent me encouraging Scriptures and meaningful books. Asked me good questions. Held self to high expectations without boasting."

—Kris Wood, 66, Oshkosh, Wisconsin,
marketplace chaplain and Director of Ministry
Operations, The Church of the Incarnation

———

"My children's great-grandmother bought all her grandchildren theology books! I have to say, those books highly influenced me as well!"

—Becki, 54, South Carolina, retired RN

## HOW ABOUT YOU?

1. What's your experience been like in telling your faith story?
2. What is one story you would like to share?
3. Who told faith stories to you?
4. If you don't want to identify an experience as spiritual, can you call it something else, like mysterious?

# NOW WHAT?

I started a graveyard search for my great-great grandmother, Christina, and ended up writing this book. Funny, but I never learned anything more about her!

You have in your hands the tools you need to be remembered. Your descendants will carry your DNA so why not give them some of your story as well?

Pass on a recipe, write a letter, share your journal, take a photo, visit your hometown, interview your dad or yourself, compile your memorable dates, research your home, carry-on traditions, tell your faith story.

Where are you going to start? One of these will fit you, and one is enough. Hopefully you'll have fun along the way and the next generations will notice your efforts and do the same. That's how legacies are always passed, one generation to the next.

Ready to tell your story? The next generation will thank you.

Letitia Suk
Letitia.suk@gmail.com

# APPENDIX ONE
## The Stories Behind the Stuff

Your heart is full of memories but so is your home. All of us have stuff; all the stuff has origin stories. I think it is fair to say that most of the origin stories are rather dull:

- Target clearance
- Rummage sale item
- Christmas gift from 2003
- Came with the house
- Don't remember

Look around your home, your mother's, your great-aunt's and you will likely find some gem of an item that comes with a great backstory. One worth passing on to the next generation. Sometimes you look at the piece your whole life and never really see it until you hear the story.

The big blue lamp was one of those items for me. A colorful table lamp with a top and bottom large glass globe was an ever-present fixture in my grandma's "front" room. The room in the farmhouse that was rarely used.

I loved the soft glow it provided when turned on. Not enough to read by but enough to draw attention to itself and become a focal point in the room. I never asked any questions about it; it just sat there like a lamp should.

Sometime in my teen years, I heard the lamp's backstory. The beautiful piece accompanied my great-great grandmother on the voyage from her homeland in Germany to the United States in the mid-1800s. At some point the bottom globe broke but a craftsman in Missouri was able to replicate that part and create a new one.

I can't imagine how it lasted on that ship. What was it packed in? Why was it so meaningful that she took a risk on bringing it? How many generations owned it before this great-grandmother?

Those answers to the questions I will never know, but I now know enough about the origin story to know why it sat proudly in my grandma's front room.

After the death of my grandmother, the lamp started residing in our living room, the one we used! The light it produced needed to be supplemented and it didn't blend well with all the other mid-century items in the room, but I loved seeing it there in the front window.

What items do you own/see that might have an interesting story? You might need to do a little investigation by asking other relatives. Questions like:

Do you remember seeing this when you were a child?
Did you ever hear anything about this?

If you have access to past photos of family gatherings you might see the item in the photo. I can clearly see the blue lamp in early Christmas photos at my grandma's home.

Since my mother's death, the lamp now sits in a corner of my living room. All my children and older grandchildren know the story of the lamp on the ship. Turns out, I have other storied items as well that never seemed special enough to talk about, but now I am.

## How to Tell the Story of Your Stuff

Consider creating a photo album or Word document, or combination of both, to share the stories of some of your memorable items. Most of us don't have that many items so this might not be a lengthy project.

Share this online document with your family members and print a hard copy to leave in an easy-to-find place. The table my blue lamp sits on has a small drawer perfect for its history. My mom made such a list of her interesting/valuable items, and that's where I found out the old rocker in my office was four generations old. My great-grandmother used to sit in it and mend her clothing.

You could also make a small card to sit next to the object like in museums. "This table was formerly owned by _____, grandparents of _____."

As you use the items, talk about them to other family members. "Can you get the placemats out of the sideboard? Did you know this piece was purchased by my grandparents when they got married in 1920?"

Don't overlook the small items. I have an enamel funnel that is quite useful, but no one would guess it is at least a hundred years old and has been in our family for at least four generations. Curious, but both of my grandmothers left me a pair of scissors. From my maternal grandmother, a pair of delicate fold-ing scissors which I now always carry in my purse. My paternal grandmother gave me a pair of quality scissors when I was about nine. Remarkably, I have managed to hang on to them all these years and use them regularly.

Don't have any family heirlooms to talk about? Start writing about the pieces you have picked up that you love. We bought a painting of the Maine shoreline on vacation in 2013. No one in our family would know that but you can find a way to tell them.

What are your family's stories behind the stuff? Give it a go to unearth them and start sharing.

# APPENDIX TWO
## What if You Really Do Want to Write Your Life Story?

"I could write a book!" is often uttered when someone has gone through a challenging season or experience. Usually, they don't! As much as we might enjoy reading an autobiography by someone we admire, or are fascinated by, the concept of writing one about ourselves is daunting. Besides, who would be interested?

By now, after exploring ten ways to tell your story to the next generation, you might realize that you have more to say. But how? There are some simple ways to make this project easier than you might imagine!

### Fill-in-the-Blank Books

A quick browse through a physical or online bookstore reveals a plethora of "fill-in-the-blank books" to tell one's personal story. Long before these became popular, my mom found one in a gift shop, and over the course of a year, filled it out for me as a gift. I was blown away by the fact that she chose to do this and by some of her answers. New details of what I thought of as an old story appeared. I made copies of the pages and gave them to my brothers.

## Writing Prompt Guides

For story tellers who want to choose their own questions from prompts, there are also many options available. One year for Christmas we gave my mother-in-law a book of questions about her life compiled by Bob Greene and D.G. Fulford called *To Our Children's Children*. Much to our surprise, she answered all the questions and returned it to us in typewritten form for the following Christmas. All the questions we would have asked and many more were answered in her book to us.

Details of her childhood and her early years as a wife and mother that we had never heard before came spilling out onto the pages. Unknown narratives about the World War II era in Chicago and her volunteer work as a "bedpan commando" stand out. Two stories about unseen spiritual protections were also fresh to her family. The prompts opened a vault of memories.

As there was initially only one copy, we made additional ones for her other eight children. The next step was to digitalize the content for the rest of the family. A few years ago, I used a printing service to create a physical book of her story and included photos of various seasons of her life. Everyone got a copy that Christmas.

## Digital Writing Prompts

A quick internet search for "writing life story prompts" will yield many options for writing your story in longhand or in a Word doc. Be sure and scroll past the sponsored links to get to the free prompts. Don't worry if you don't like or can't relate to some of the questions. Choose the ones that appeal to you.

### Subscription Story Programs

A life story subscription program that is quite user friendly and well known is Storyworth. One of my friends told me excitedly about a gift she received from her kids. She explained that each week she receives a question about her life via email. To answer the question, you simply respond to the email with your answer.

I decided to ask for it from my kids too for my birthday. The first question arrived, "What were your grandparents like?" and I was off and running! I have loved these questions, and my kids regularly report, "Oh Mom, I didn't know that about you." Sometimes I feel the same as a long-forgotten memory bubbles up to the surface.

If you don't like the question, you can choose another or make up your own. In addition, you can also attach photos to illustrate the story. You can write as much or little as you wish and each week your answer can be sent to whomever you choose. At the end of the year, you get a hardbound copy of your stories which is part of the subscription.

Who would ever think to ask what your next-door neighbors were like when you were a child? I had so much fun with that one that I sent it to my brothers too, as, of course, they were also their neighbors. Sometimes I miss a week but then later catch up.

After renewing my annual subscription four times, I ordered the published book of all the stories I had sent in and loved how it came out!

Storyworth.com

### Freehand Writing

Of course, there is always the option to pull out a notebook or open a blank document and start writing. Your story is written however you wish in whatever style, order, or length you desire. This is how life stories were always written before the internet age with all the available resources.

### Publishing Your Book

If you choose to publish your writings for your family, there are resources available. Your local printer can bind your work, or you can engage a printing service for a more polished look. An internet search will provide options for self-publishing. A ringed binder is just fine too.

# APPENDIX THREE
## The Thanksgiving Journal

It is Thanksgiving morning of *any* year, the one day in the calendar year when our family eats breakfast in the living room. Crowded around a round card table precariously laden with fancy dishes and silverware owned by previous generations, champagne glasses filled with eggnog, and specialty foods, we give thanks.

While the once-a-year special egg dish is passed, we start recounting our blessings of the past year. The new babysitting job, the fun summer vacation, Grandma's successful surgery, the fact that the basement *didn't* flood . . . from the spectacular to the mundane, we are grateful.

What has turned out to be one of our most treasured family rituals is that we *remember* all these thanks. Only because, as the self-appointed secretary, I write it all down. Not nicely at all but rather fast and furious, in between sips of tea, so as not to slow down the flow.

By the end of breakfast, a long sheet of paper is filled with cryptic notes and initials of who was grateful for what. Later that weekend I will carefully transcribe this year's thanks into

the *Thanksgiving Journal,* a simple fabric-lined journal purchased at a bookstore a long time ago, which we designated for
this purpose.

After coffee refills and table chitchat, we pull out the journal and read the entries of what we were thankful for in years
past, going back to 1982 when we started the tradition. In the
early years, we read ALL the entries from each year but more
recently have decided that each family member can choose a
year to read. If we have extra time before the turkey needs to
get put in the oven, we read a few more years. The early years
are most often chosen!

Much laughter ensues as we recall a four-year-old's grateful-
ness for a new trike, the year we got our winter coats at a great
garage sale, the addition of a guinea pig to the family circle. We
also remember the family triumphs: the completion of a project
at work, the beginning of a new baby-sitting job, the mastery of
a hard piece on the violin, or the winning Little League team.

Some people in our circle show up often in our journal: the
teacher that taught all four of our kids, the children's pastor at
church, grandmas and grandpas and our close friends who live
two doors away. Friends who have moved on are also remembered:
the upstairs neighbors who provided the playmates, the best friend
from kindergarten, the work colleague who was so helpful.

Vacations of each year are always recalled with thanks—
Niagara Falls, the ocean, the campsites, and the family van that
took us to all those places.

Not just the fun items are listed, but the harder stuff of life
is transformed into thanks in the pages of the journal as well.
We're thankful that our friend who died is in heaven; grateful
that mom's car accident wasn't worse; glad for the new bike to
replace the one that was stolen.

In addition, I also record the names of the guests who join us each year. Often a collection of who is available as our families don't live nearby. *Remember John and Sue? Whatever happened to Mark? Who is Terry? Wow, the Bowkers have come seventeen times!*

By the end of breakfast, we are not only full of the special foods but also of rich memories of fun times, friends along the way, places we have been, and God's faithfulness. We are now ready to spend the rest of the day with family and friends, details of which such as the weather, special treats, new games, and assorted tidbits such as the year the plumbing backed up will also be recorded in the journal.

Later in the day, the same card table will hold a jigsaw puzzle for old and new friends to work on while drinking hot cider and waiting for the traditional dinner. Following the feast is a group walk around the block and spirited game playing. One of the beauties of Thanksgiving is that we all know the script!

In this season of our life, we occasionally travel to visit family over this beloved holiday. The journal comes along, and the tradition is carried on at someone else's table. By the following Monday it will return to its place on the shelf next to the one that holds the Christmas memories. We remember what we have written.

# APPENDIX FOUR
## Additional Stories

Do you enjoy reading about the experiences of others in telling their stories? Here are more to inspire you!

### On Keeping a Journal

"I didn't start out intending to journal every day straight for twelve years, but that's what happened. Keeping up with the journal was probably most challenging during the first few weeks of having a child, but even in those days, I just had to find a regular time that worked for me.

Sometimes, when I talk about my journaling practice, people sigh and say, 'Gosh, I wish I had the discipline to journal every day.' And I always say, 'No! It's not about self-discipline! It's just a thing I have to do!' Journaling is really good for my soul."

—Ann Boyd, 49, Chicago, Illinois, editor

———

"I think I started keeping a journal in junior high, so about twenty-five years ago. Most days are just a few sentences about the facts of the day. I've been 'bullet journaling' for a year now. It's so much faster and simpler for me. I think it helps me record the more important things that are happening. I try not to focus on negative things the way I used to."

—Beth Genenbacher, 44, Quincy, Illinois, finance associate

## On Photos

"A few years ago, my aunt gave me framed individual black-and-white photos of my grandparents when they were young, early in their marriage."

—Sarah Schwartz (previously cited)

———

"Every Christmas Eve, my siblings and I give our parents a new calendar with photos of the grandchildren and our families. Last year, we reminisced while looking at probably fifteen calendars or more that Mom had saved over the years."

—Beth Peter O'Neill (previously cited)

———

"At Christmas, I plan to give each of our four children a thumb drive with the family slides I have carefully combed through. I also fit about ten hours of VHS home video on there too."

—Brian Chaplin (previously cited)

## On Traditions

"For me, I feel that I am respecting and honoring the generation that has come before me. Grandma and Grandpa, and Great-Grandma and Grandpa have gone out of their way to follow through on these traditions. I will, too, to keep the story going forward."

—Michelene Reed, 61, Kenosha, Wisconsin, foster mom

———

"In my family growing up, my dad worked shift work and always had to work Christmas day. So, we all went to church together on the Eve. Somehow my parents always forgot to grab something after we were all loaded in the car for church. This was Santa's time to drop everything quickly under the tree."

—Jessica Lucas, 46, Wheaton, Illinois, counselor

———

"Since my husband and I are ministers, we are at church with our boys on Christmas Eve. There is a tradition at David's church that our son Christopher, who is on the autism spectrum, comes in at the end of service, and he and David and the whole congregation sing, 'We Wish You a Merry Christmas.' Everybody looks forward to it, and it's been going on for the last nine years."

—Rev. Mary Armstrong-Reiner (previously cited)

———

"On Christmas Eve, the children would go to their rooms so the angels could come and decorate the live Christmas tree complete with real candles. Christmas started after midnight Mass, always with sitting still until a set of German and Italian songs had been played from the stereo."

—Riccardo Ferrante, 60, Brunswick, MD,
Digital services management

————

"We have a tree-trimming party! I put up the tree and lights, but then we invite friends over to help us decorate. It's fun to share all the history of our ornaments with people. Then I make a fun dinner and dessert. One year, I invited my daughter's choir friends and they sang a cappella the whole time while decorating. Magical!"

—Ronnell Kay Gibson, 52, Fond du Lac,
Wisconsin, graphic designer

————

"I make a 'soda cake' for my kids. It's on our table the morning of their birthday. In today's world where you have parties on a weekend or when other family members are available, I always wanted to make sure they felt special on the actual day they were born. Most of the time it has the child's favorite soda, snacks, candy, and an item or two that they can play with or a movie to watch—something so it makes celebrating them extra special."

—Christine Tourney, 44, Hull, Illinois, account executive

————

"A tradition in our family is observing St. Martin's Day, which is celebrated in many parts of Europe. We had some neighbors from Spain and Germany in our old apartment building who invited us to walk with lanterns around our nearby rose garden, sing some songs in German, and then come back to their apartment for hot cocoa and Toblerone. When we moved into our own home, for a few years we would throw a big lantern party and do a parade in our neighborhood. It was fun. We stopped doing it as our kids got older, but this year, we decided to revive it and invite some friends with four younger kids over for a meal and a low-key celebration like the one that got us hooked in the first place."

—Julia Moore (previously cited)

## On Recipes and Food

"I created a small cookbook for a family reunion back in 1997. I asked for old family recipes and then denoted those with a special symbol in the cookbook. I also welcomed new favorites."

—Melissa Ramer (previously cited)

———

"It wouldn't be Thanksgiving without my grandma's homemade noodles. My dad took over making them after his mom passed, and he taught my niece, so the tradition will continue!"

—Sharyn Kopf, 60, Bellefontaine, Ohio, newspaper reporter and freelance writer/editor

———

"One year my father forgot to buy the food for Christmas dinner, and we didn't realize it until we went to make it. The only store that was still open didn't have many options but did have the fixings for meatloaf. That began the tradition of having meatloaf for Christmas dinner every year. I miss this a lot."

—Rebecca Weber, 45, Chicago, Illinois, animal care steward at animal shelter

―――――――

"Food is our family's love language! Here are a few of the recipes on repeat for holidays and reunions: drinkable custard, Blarney Stones (little cakes rolled in peanuts or coconut), yeast rolls, macaroni and cheese, bonbons, peanut brittle, deviled eggs, fresh apple cake, Ooey Gooey Butter Bars, Texas Sheet Cake, cranberry salad/relish, mashed potato salad, fried pies, pound cake, baked beans, fried chicken, homemade ice cream."

—Kathy Carlton Willis, 61, Tyler,
Texas, speaker, coach, author

―――――――

"I think the unique to us were (Bohemian) dumplings and sauerkraut with our turkey for Thanksgiving. I was in college when I discovered that others ate mashed potatoes as a side. My great aunt Joan made the pierogis, and, of course, there was no recipe written down. We asked her to make them for us while we watched, measured, and recorded what she did. Years later after she had passed, my sister and I started making the pierogis every year from this record. We then kept a little notebook, called the Pierogi Chronicles, where we kept notes on what worked and didn't, until we achieved pierogis that were almost as good as Aunt Joan's!"

—Lisa Plefka Haskin (previously cited)

―――――――

"On the German side of my family, we always had multiple meats at every holiday. On my dad's side, I spent a lot of time with my English and Scotch Irish 'Grandmommie' Bird, my great-grandmother, when I was little. She was an amazing scratch cook. Her pies, cakes, hash, chicken and dumplings, and fried chicken were legendary. She raised children during the Depression, and a grandson (my dad) during WWII. Even though she and Grandaddy owned a grocery store, food was scarce back then. Sometimes, dinner was white rice with milk and a little sugar on top. She made it for me as a little girl, and I loved it. I still make it and think of her and my dad."

—Christine Bird Douglas, 59, Highland Park, Illinois,
Chief Grant Officer at a nonprofit that serves victims
of domestic violence and human trafficking

———————

"My mom was famous for her angel food cakes and frequently brought them to family reunions. She made them from scratch and didn't use an electric mixer, beating them by hand. Her apple pies were wonderful! She learned from Grandma Smith and taught me. She didn't have a recipe; she just knew how. She finally wrote down the recipe as best she could, and it took me ten years to perfect it. I have it down now. I love these recipes. They keep me connected to my mom and grandma, as they were grandma's recipes originally. I want to pass them down to my daughter."

—Phyllis Vaughn, 68, Winchester, Virginia, retired

———————

"The Black side of my family had many family recipes. My dad loves the raisin pie and icebox cookies with walnuts that his grandmother used to make. We also usually make a few family soul food recipes for the holidays. Usually, my mom makes greens, and sometimes my sister or I make baked mac and cheese. My grandmother always made 7-Up cake and chitterlings for the holidays along with a turkey, gelled cranberries, plus a full soul food meal. I don't really care for the cake or chitlins, so we haven't continued that tradition. My Irish grandmother was not an exceptionally good cook, but she was a wonderful baker and made delicious donuts and cream puffs as well as fudge every Christmas. I finally mastered fudge a few years ago."

—Meegan Dugan Adell, 47, Evanston,
Illinois, public policy researcher

"I have been adding family recipes to Createmycookbook.com. I have included photos of the littles cooking through the years. I also add a bit of history of the recipe like the mini meatloaves I made while a tornado was raging above and through our apartment. I add the date of when I found the recipe and tips about the making of the recipe, if needed. I asked my husband to choose Bible verses for the cookbook, and I add one to each page. One of our sons mentioned that he would prefer the recipes laminated and in a three-ring binder. That surely works for me—less costly and easier to use. Of course, the recipes are all on the computer for easy access."

—Andrea Cain, 72, Bolingbrook,
Illinois, children's pastor/teacher

"My husband is from India, and his mom would send us her secret spice mix that makes his curries better than anyone else. She passed the secret down to her daughter before she passed. My daughter is hoping to be the next to carry it on."

—Sarah Kodavatikanti, 50, Skokie,
Illinois, church administrator

---

"My mother made filled cookies. Sugar cookie dough on the top and bottom with raisins and nuts cooked in sugary flour in between. We carried these in our lard bucket (lunch pails), but now my grandkids come to make these cookie/pies because they carry our family tradition and just taste good. The recipe is in my mother's handwriting on the back of an envelope used to save on paper. Priceless."

—Cleo Lampos (previously cited)

## On Homes and Neighborhoods

"We did not know it until our final walk through, six-and-a-half years ago, but we live in Orville Redenbacher's first home in Valparaiso, Indiana. He's kind of a big deal around here! Orville's children wrote on the rafters in the attic, which was their secret hideaway."

—Sherri Seward, 58, Valparaiso, Indiana,
musician/music educator

## On Interviewing

"When my grandmother entered hospice two years ago, I made a trip to see her specifically with this in mind. It was actually really difficult to start the conversation, and while I'd been told that I should record our conversation, that felt weird and intrusive. So instead, I took copious notes as she shared big moments of faith and family from her life, and when she died quite quickly (only a few weeks later—we all thought she had months left) I wrote it all up and emailed it to all of our family. My parents also made copies and distributed among her friends, and we had it available at her memorial service."

—Stephanie Register (previously cited)

———

"I'm a first generation American to parents who were born and raised in Nassau, Bahama. That being said, many of my interviews took place over the phone. My Aunt Nora was our family Historian. I learned so much from her. My only wish was that she lived long enough for me to have time to gather more wonderful stories about our family; stories like finding out my Grandfather was the Captain of the Bahama Navy. Aunt Nora died at the young age of ninety-two."

—Annette Mota (already cited)

———

"When I moved my kids to the Midwest, I chose the location so they could be near to my grandma (their great-grandmother) and hear some of her stories of growing up on a farm in Central Illinois, like riding a horse around the farm."

—Katherine O'Brien, 59, Dubuque, Iowa, consultant

———

"My family has a Marco Polo channel we use to stay connected. We bought a book called *Interview with Grandpa* and my kids would regularly ask a question from the book then my dad (and sometimes mom) would answer the questions. It was a fun way to capture memories and stories for all of us to hear."

—Keri Kersten, 52, Des Plaines, Illinois, manager, learning and organization development

———

"I interviewed my grandma when in college, and my oldest child interviewed her living grandparents and great-grandparents in person for a project."

—Tiffany Colter, 48, Toledo, Ohio, business owner

———

"I've been doing this with my dad. I'm using the record feature on my phone, and my husband is using a feature of Office online to create a transcript for each recording. Then I work with each transcript to make corrections and fill in details. I plan to compile this into some type of document or book that family members can access and order copies for themselves."

—Wendy Hinote Lanier, 60, Lindale, Texas, author

———

"I interviewed three of my grandparents before they passed. I asked them all kinds of questions about their childhood and their ancestors. The videos are now family treasures!"

—Kenneth Maresco, 63, Centreville, Virginia, pastor

———

"I recorded my dad on tape as he talked about his childhood and life. My sister had interviewed both my parents, which has since been transcribed. My daughter made a scrapbook for her grandma's seventy-fifth birthday and spent many hours gleaning family history from her to put in the book."

—Ruth Madziarczyk (previously cited)

---

"I interviewed my grandmother on the phone about their WWII experience in a Japanese internment camp. I edited and typed it up and sent it to her. She was very pleased."

—Ellen Kipnis Glatt, 74, Skokie, Illinois, co-restaurateur

---

"I interviewed, on 1988 video technology, my mom's mom. I cherish her stories of living in Alaska and her love of salmon fishing—her views of life and wisdom passed on to me. The video is now digitalized."

—Kay Masse, 69, Arvada, Colorado, Colorado notary public

---

"I had a great-great-aunt who had an amazing life as a physician and colonel during/after WWII, working with General McArthur. She wrote her autobiography, which I just had printed/ bound for my mom's birthday."

—Vivien Alsberg, 63, Skokie, Illinois, registered nurse

---

"I have a huge number of relatives on my paternal grandparents' side and have photos going back to the early 1900s. We have recordings from interviews with some of my aunts and uncles."

—Marge Carhart, 87, Island Lake, Illinois, retired

## On Traveling

"I wanted my husband, Tim, to see the farmhouse where I grew up in Australia. Figured that it was deserted now due to how wrecked it looked outside. Snuck in and took a tour—oops, there was food in the kitchen, a fire burning, and definite signs of life."

—Jessica Dunn, 36, Kuranda, Queensland, Australia, pastor

———

Although we were both from Arizona, the day my husband, Wayne, proposed to me was when we were driving around Minnesota visiting all the churches his family members were either baptized, married, or buried. The last church we stopped at had a history with Wayne's family as they were part of a group of immigrants who settled in the area and organized the parish. A log cabin church was built in 1856 where his great-grandparents were married and his grandfather was baptized. It was destroyed by fire in 1864 and rebuilt with the help of his family in 1866 out of brick and stone. As the parish grew, more room was needed and the church as it stands today was completed in 1907.

We arrived at the beautiful church and Wayne and I were the only two people inside. We proceeded down the aisle of the church and sat in the first row closest to the altar. Then he popped the question!

As we were exiting the church we saw the priest and told him we just got engaged in the church. We explained why we were here and that we would marry in our parish back in Phoenix. He asked if he could bless our engagement and our future marriage. Of course, I knew then we would be married for life!"

—Julie Schaak, Phoenix, AZ

———

"All my life I had heard 'so and so was buried in the Wylds Cemetery.' As an adult, I've been there several times and seen markers for my paternal grandfather, an uncle who died as a child from malaria, an aunt who was killed in a tornado at age eleven, a great-aunt who died after being kicked by a cow, a fourth great-grandfather (who owned the cemetery), and numerous other relatives. Sadly, it is on private property and untended, so each time I go, I can find fewer markers. I love family history, and this makes me feel connected to those family members."

—Ruth Madziarczyk (previously cited)

———

"I've driven the route to my old school when I've been in back in the area. The school isn't there anymore, but I want my daughter to see the place. My mom loved to show me the house she was born in which was wiped out in the '93 flood. She showed me her school and the places in Hannibal that she remembered from growing up there."

—Phyllis Vaughn (previously cited)

———

"I wanted to show the kids my childhood environment and show them I hadn't always been a farmer. My grade school, junior high, and the alley I haunted every day—it's a lot of memories all packed into a small area."

—John Peter Shaddle, 74, Plano, Illinois, retired

———

"As I get older, I'm feeling more and more like there's a part of me that's anchored to that place and time. It might be odd, but

I'm more aware of it when it's a place I'm back in than when I reunite with old friends. I am more still in those places. With old friends, there's such wonderful conversation that sometimes overshadows that stillness."

—Riccardo Ferrante (previously cited)

"Going back reminds me of happy times as a kid. When I was younger, my parents were separated and divorced. I didn't fully understand divorce, but I like seeing where my dad lived in the city and remembering shared times with him. Driving by my childhood home and street and other key places just gives me warm vibes of happy times with my childhood friends and neighbors who gave me love and nurtured me. I'm forever grateful, so when I go back there, it just makes me feel good."

—Vicki A Borgman, 55, Des Plaines, Illinois,
long-term disability specialist

## On Letters

"I saved all the letters from when my husband, Mike, was in the Navy. Someday my great-grandchildren will enjoy them. We have letters from Mom and Dad when Dad was overseas during WWII. All the family history is why we save letters. Letters can be like reading a person's soul."

—M. J. Creger, 73, Palmyra, Missouri, retired

"I have letters from my great-grandparents to my grandmother. I love and cherish them."

—Susan R. Lawrence, 74, Des Moines, Iowa, writer

———

"I have a series of letters between my aunt and uncle when they were dating and he was overseas in WWII. It is record of their very special courtship, and I cherish them."

—Nancy Voorhees, 59, Liberty Lake, Washington, writer

———

"I never throw away a letter. I believe so strongly that people matter and so does the written word. This year, I've challenged myself to write and mail fifty-two letters as God leads."

—Casey Butler, 45, Wisconsin Dells,
Wisconsin, photographer/caregiver/writer

———

"Ted and I wrote letters while we were dating. He had come back home to farm, and I was in college. We still have them all."

—Sarah Schwartz (previously cited)

———

"I write letters because some occasions are more deserving of a letter versus an email. I keep letters from loved ones in the photo albums with the photos."

—Marie Davies, 66, St. Louis, Missouri,
bed-and-breakfast specialist/innkeeper

———

"I have the love letters my great-grandparents sent each other when they were courting back in the late 1800s. They're so fun and romantic. I started using them for a novel."

—Sharyn Kopf (previously cited)

———

"I have my mother's letters to my grandparents when she first married. And the telegrams my parents sent to each other including my father's proposal to my mom and her response (yes, repeated to fill character limit)."

—Myrle Croasdale, 62, Buffalo, Minnesota,
copywriter and journalist

———

"I have a very special set of handwritten letters from my mother, written between 1956–57, when she was traveling in Europe before I was born. They turned up in my grandfather's retirement home in a forgotten suitcase half a century later—long after he had passed away. Grandpa had been the last recipient, and these were circular, to be passed around to all the family in turn. I have retyped them and put them in a notebook. They were precious to me since my mom had died when I was very young, and I had not known about this time in her life."

—Debra Dimon Davis (previously cited)

———

"I have a lot of old letters from a second cousin. We didn't know each other until we were fifteen years old. When her grandmother came for my grandfather's funeral, she told me about her granddaughter who was the same age, showed me pics and told me she would have her write to me. We've corresponded ever since."

—Judith A Cox, 74, Hull, Illinois, retired AT&T
operator, bank teller, activity director, teacher

———

"During COVID, I read all my mother's letters to and from my father before they were married in 1930. Then the letters were from my grandmother to my mother who was living in Wyoming during the Great Depression. I read Mom's diary. I have a great appreciation for the Greatest Generation."

—Cleo Lampos (previously cited)

## On Faith

"My parents lived their faith. I saw it every day in everything they did. Of course, they also took me to church every time there was an opportunity, but the real lesson was what I saw them devoted to, and that was God."

—Ruth Madziarczyk (previously cited)

———

"Family showed me their faith by living it out. My mom and dad made faith a central part of our lives. My grandpa became very committed to God in his later years through attending Mass almost daily and to his care for the nuns by taking them eggs and food. My aunt and uncle invited me to a Christian event that changed my life forever. I am thankful for our family who helped me through tough times and always showed me Jesus' love."

—Rev. Mary Armstrong-Reiner (previously cited)

———

"My parents 'lived' church, they did not just 'go to church.' One of my youngest memories is sitting on a high stool in the church kitchen in the basement of a 150-year-old church as the women prepared meals/cookies for Sunday mornings. But the biggest place they lived their faith is in caring for my disabled sister at a time there was no educational support. Both my parents and a whole church community supported our family. I am forever grateful for these stories, but I could fill a book with examples!"

—Patricia Milazzo (previously cited)

# ACKNOWLEDGMENTS

This book was born somewhere in Kansas on a long train trip between Chicago, Illinois, and Gallup, New Mexico. Thank you, Amtrak, for providing the perfect setting and enough time to think about storytelling for the next generation.

The title showed up later during a conversation with my husband who came up with the final version. Thank you, Tom, for your unwavering support and constant cheerleading for this project. And all my other endeavors! I love you so much.

My beloved friends never seemed to tire of hearing me talk about the power of story. Thank you, Pat, Cindy, Cathy, Eloise, Theresa, Alison, Jess, Cheryll, Jane, Ann, and more.

My children: Jesh, Gabe, Selah, and Christa are the direct beneficiaries of all my stories. Thank you for letting me try out all ten methods with you over your lifetimes. Pass it on! To my brothers, Brad and Mark who have been the witnesses of my story for the longest.

To all my contributors who answered my questions on social media and shared a snippet of your stories which ended up in these pages, thank you.

Other writers in my circle also lent advice, perspective, and practical tips: Michelle, Kathy, Ginger (gone too soon), and the Write-to-Publish community.

Thank you to Hope who said, "send it in" and Victoria who said "yes" on my birthday!

For all of you I asked to pray for this project, thank you.

Thank you to Jesus. In you I live and move and have my being.

# ABOUT THE AUTHOR

Letitia Suk (Tish) invites women to chase the intentional life. She writes and speaks of renewal and restoration, offering platters of hope to women in each season of life. Her blend of humor, stories, and grace propels audiences towards a fresh experience of God.

Tish is also a retreat guide in the Chicago area. Her popular guided personal retreats, called "Slow Dance with Jesus," are based on her book *Getaway with God*. During these 24 hours, women unplug from stress and plug into rest, connect with God, and re-order their lives.

For fun she likes to collect family stories, walk by Lake Michigan, browse resale shops, drink tea with a book in hand, and make up new family traditions to enjoy with her husband, Tom. Hanging out with their four adult children and many grands in the backyard are the best times. Her favorite mode of transportation is the train, the longer ride the better!

Tish decided to be a writer when she was a girl and years later started out with magazine articles. She is the author of *100 Need-to-Know Tips for Moms of Tweens and Teens* (Ellie Claire/ Hachette, 2019); *Getaway with God: The Everywoman's Guide to Personal Retreat* (Kregel, 2016); and *Rhythms of Renewal* (This-JOY Books, 2009). You can find her at Letitiasuk.com.